were you
raised
by wolves?

were you raised by wolves?

and seven other crucial questions to ask the one you just might marry

TOBEN HEIM

Kregel
Publications

Were You Raised by Wolves? And Seven Other Crucial Questions to Ask the One You Just Might Marry

© 2010 by Toben Heim

Published by Kregel Publications, a division of Kregel, Inc., P.O. Box 2607, Grand Rapids, MI 49501.

ISBN 978-0-8254-2750-3

Printed in the United States of America

10 11 12 13 14 / 5 4 3 2 1

To Steve and Barbara Uhlmann,
whose passion for healthy marriages
brought this book into being

Contents

Introduction 9

1. Were You Raised by Wolves?
   Families of Origin 17

2. Are You Talkin' to Me? Are You Talkin' to *ME*?
   Communication. 31

3. Do You Fight Dirty?
   Conflict Resolution 43

4. Do You Take Plastic?
   Money and Finances. 57

5. Why Aren't Your Friends Normal?
   Friendships and Community 69

6. What the Heck Is a Yoke?
   Faith and Religion 85

7. Is "Barista" a Profession?
   Career and Calling 99

8. Minivan or Mini Cooper?
   Children and Family Life 109

Conclusion: Are You Seeing What I'm Seeing? . . . 117

Introduction

was nineteen years old when I got engaged. I asked Joanne to marry me when she was eighteen, the night before her high school graduation. (Don't worry, her parents have since recovered.) At the time, I thought I knew everything I needed to know about Joanne in order to make an informed decision to ask her to spend the rest of her life with me. Beyond that, I thought we both possessed the necessary stuff to produce a successful marriage. After all, we really loved each other, we had fun together, we had lots in common, and our families were similar enough to make us think that we had models in common that would serve us well.

We were a bit of a unique case (as most engagements are) because we were so young. And because we spent almost two years as an engaged couple before we tied the knot. In those two years, what we didn't know about each other and about relationships became clear. Fortunately for us, we were committed to working through a lot of these shortcomings before we walked down the aisle. I'd love to say that the process was easy and that we stepped into marriage and bliss followed. But the truth is, it was a lot of work. And it takes consistent vigilance on our part to continue to learn and grow together.

WORK AT IT

Work is a natural part of all relationships, at almost every stage. It takes work to figure out how to be a good friend. It takes effort to be a good child to your parents or a good sibling or a good employee. It takes concerted effort in almost any relationship that counts to help it be all that it could be. Without that effort relationships grow stagnant and sometimes even fail.

And why is that? Why aren't relationships easier? After all, God has made it clear that he desires us to live in all kinds of relationships. He wants us to live in community. He desires for us to be involved in a church, to have close friends, and to maybe even marry. But at the same time, we are hardwired to have difficulty in most of these relationships. Here's why: most of us, way down deep, are selfish. And if you want to know the source of that, well, you are going to have to go back to the fall (not the season, but the fall back in the garden of Eden). Remember that story? You can find it in Genesis 3. Eve is tempted by the serpent and eats from the Tree of Knowledge of Good and Evil. Then she takes the fruit to Adam and he does the same. In doing so they created separation from God and took on all kinds of human characteristics that stay with us to this day . . . including selfishness.

Difficulty in relationships is a real bummer. After all, if we are hardwired to desire relationships, why can't we also be wired to make them easy, rewarding, and beneficial? Well, difficulty is a reality in our lives, and that's never more evident than in our primary relationship—the one with God. You are likely familiar with the idea of the God-shaped void in our lives, and that we have a compulsion to fill that void with something, anything.

Even when we realize that God is the only one who can truly fill us up, we often continue to try and fill that void with things that will never satisfy.

So if we are hardwired to need God but, since the fall, determined to try and replace him with something else, how much more likely is it that even though we need relationships, we will be innately unable to do them right? And the tough news is that this is especially true of our primary relationship here on Earth—the one with a potential or eventual spouse. Same reasons mentioned above apply here: our desire to serve ourselves outweighs our desire to serve another.

But there is hope! Among all that God has given us, he has blessed us with the ability to learn. We have the capacity to learn how he can come into our lives and fill that empty space. And likewise we have the ability to learn how to have a healthy, productive, and meaningful relationship with another significant person in our lives.

THE TARGET

Helping readers to have healthy, productive, and meaningful relationships is the ultimate purpose of this book. But I'll come at it from a different angle—offering you the questions instead of the answers. A number of books out there will bluntly tell you what you need to do in order to have a good relationship. I shy away from that approach, opting instead to ask questions to get you thinking about what you need to know, how you need to act, and what you need to learn to put your best foot forward in the most important earthly relationship you will experience.

Sure, there may be a little teaching along the way, but each person who reads this book is unique, so coming up with a single set of instructions won't meet everyone's needs. Yes, the end target is the same for all of us, but the way each of us gets there might look a little different. So I will give you questions to consider, and a justification for why these questions are important. You can choose to answer these questions by yourself, you can go through them with a significant other, or you can tackle this content in a small-group setting. Maybe you'll want to get a journal where you can capture some of your thoughts and answers.

If you work through the book with your significant other, don't try to tackle all these topics at once. It would be overwhelming to sit down and work through this book in a weekend! That's not realistic and would put an amazing amount of strain on a relationship. Try tackling these topics one at a time over the course of a few weeks. After all, you're not in a hurry—you are learning about each other, how you're wired, and what matters to you. If you really love someone, this is a fun journey.

Keep in mind that you are going to have questions for your significant other that aren't in the book. So write down whatever additional questions you might have and ask them too. Make sure you give each other enough time to wrestle through these questions. You need to set aside a few hours of quality time so that you can really unpack the issues.

GROUND RULES

When you work through these topics and questions, make sure that you listen well—you owe that to your significant other.

You can expect that they will pay you the same courtesy. After all, you're talking about important stuff here. Make sure that you ask clarifying questions so you really understand what your significant other thinks about a given topic.

Oftentimes you will get a much better and more thoughtful response if you are willing to answer questions first, even if they're not posed to you. Volunteer the information and then ask, "So, what about you?" The first person to respond sets the depth meter on the response. Say you want to ask a question about finances. If you start by volunteering that you "have a little bit of credit card debt," you can expect a similarly shallow response. But if you go into detail about the amount of debt, the nature of it, and why you have it, it is reasonable to expect that your significant other will respond in kind. However, if you are volunteering quite a bit and your partner comes back with shallow answers to deep questions, then you have the right to push a little.

Some of these subjects are going to be hard for you or your significant other to talk about. For example, not everyone had a great childhood. Sometimes talking about what life was like growing up in our families is hard to do. When you run into one of these topics, take your time. Be patient. Don't push too hard. Be encouraging and gentle when you hit a sore spot. Remember that you can't expect your significant other to answer questions that you yourself are not willing to answer.

Just because topics or questions are difficult doesn't mean that they are off-limits. For example, if you are talking about faith and your significant other says something like, "That's private," that's an unacceptable answer and requires you to gently prod to figure out what the hang-up is. Ideally, both you and your significant other will read this book and be prepared to talk about the tough stuff, but if it's just you who's reading, you might have more work cut out for you as you seek to unearth your own thoughts on these tough topics. But the reality is, if you are going to get engaged or possibly married, you deserve to have answers.

You deserve to know your significant other's thoughts on these topics because they are critical to your future and your success as an engaged or married couple. If you don't uncover potential conflicts early on, they will come up at some point in the relationship, guaranteed. You don't want to be in a serious relationship where your partner is closed off, secretive, unco-operative, or inauthentic. If you have problems discussing these topics with your significant other, don't expect a wedding ring to clear up the problem. You are going to be the same person going into a marriage as you were before the relationship got serious.

So you need to talk about the topics in this book. It may be uncomfortable to tackle issues that seem far down the road, but trust me, if you are anticipating a serious long-term relationship with the possibility of engagement and marriage, you might as well jump in with both feet.

JOURNEY OF DISCOVERY

One great way to think about your relationship is that it is a journey of discovery. You have an incredible opportunity in a significant relationship to learn all sorts of things. What you may not be expecting is that you can learn all sorts of things about yourself. So many of the questions have as much to do with how you are wired, what you are looking for, and what your needs are as they have to do with your significant other. Self-knowledge is critically important to the success of any relationship.

This book provides ample opportunity to learn about the person you are falling in love with. When you really love someone you want to know that person well, right? You want to discover what is true about them and what makes them tick. So learn about yourself, and then take an adventurous spirit into your discovery of this person you care so much about.

My goal for you is simple: in considering these questions, I hope you will walk into this significant relationship with your eyes wide open, knowing what you need to learn (both about yourself and about your "other") in order to have a great relationship, one that will stand the test of time and the travails that accompany all relationships.

A great relationship is possible, and God has given us the capacity to learn how to do it. So enjoy the questions. I hope they reveal a few things to you that maybe you hadn't thought of before and, in that discovery, you will find a path to the happiness that can come through engagement and marriage.

DISCOVERY QUESTIONS TO GET YOU STARTED

1. Do you agree that great relationships are a learned skill?
2. What do you think of the statement, "We are hardwired for self-centered relationships and other-centered ones don't come naturally"? How have you seen this play out in your life?

3. Describe other relationships you have invested a lot of time and effort in. What have been the benefits of your investment?

4. Have you ever tried to fill your God-shaped void with anything other than God? What was the result?

5. What was something you had to work hard to learn? How might that experience of learning impact your desire to learn how to do romantic relationships right?

6. What is your expectation as you read this book? What is your desired outcome?

7. Can you identify any topics that might be challenging for you to address as a couple? What makes them so challenging?

CHAPTER 1

Were You Raised by Wolves?

FAMILIES OF ORIGIN

I wish I had known how he was raised.
I just thought everyone was raised the way I was.
Silly, I know. I could fully take care of myself;
I was totally self-sufficient prior to
marriage. I got married and found out that I had
to teach my husband how to crack an egg.
He came from an old-school background
where the woman did everything
in the home. I came from a family that broke
everything up into a team activity.

—JANET, NEVADA

An old axiom says, "If you don't know your history, you are bound to repeat it." How true! Besides our own personal histories, we can expect the same to hold true for a significant other.

If we don't know where they come from and who their models are, we are missing out on some important facts and information about this person. But first, let's start with you. After all, it wouldn't be fair to ask questions about where your significant other comes from if you aren't prepared to answer those questions yourself.

So, where do you come from? This isn't a geography question. You need to uncover the ways in which you were brought up—the biases that were instilled in you, the patterns of behavior that you have adopted, and the way you view and act in relationships. A lot of this comes from the way you saw your parents relate to each other. Were they affectionate toward each other? Did they handle conflict well? Did they respect each other? Your parents, whether they were good parents or bad, provide a model for you. You need to understand what they modeled so you can see those traits in yourself, which means you need to become a self-observer. We'll talk more about becoming a self-observer later in this chapter.

WEIRD HABITS

It is safe to say of your significant other that a lot of their behavior, especially in the context of your relationship, can be explained. That's the good news! When Joanne and I were engaged she did some weird things. At least they were weird to me. Of course she did some of these things when we were dating, but they somehow became more pronounced after we decided to get married.

The strangest thing that she did related to communication, and more specifically, communication under stress or disagreement. When the discussion would get heated, when we were about to have a full-blown argument, Joanne would stop talking. And I mean stop. It was weird to me because in my family we disagreed, um . . . vocally. We had no problem mixing it up and certainly none of us would have thought of shutting down in the face of a disagreement. We were too busy battling for our point of view. But that wasn't Joanne.

· · · · · · · · ·

First and most importantly, I wish that I'd known how past relationships could affect our marriage.

—STACY, NORTH DAKOTA

· · · · · · · · ·

So, there we would be, with the emotional temperature running high, and Joanne would go silent. It made me crazy! More than anything I wanted her to argue with me. That's what I was used to. But that's not how arguments were handled in Joanne's home. When things would heat up, her dad would often settle the dispute without leaving room for discussion or debate. Dad laid down the law and that was that. So for her, there was no reason to keep debating.

Now, as much as it drove me crazy that she would go silent, understanding that this is how she was brought up at least explained it and helped me to understand that this was a learned behavior. She wasn't just doing it to drive me crazy; it was what was natural to her. Over time, we were able to make changes and compromises because we both understood that we had family history that made us communicate differently.

All of us come into relationships with a sense of the "right way" things should happen. This is true for almost all our interactions, big or small. Some of those behaviors might be endearing. For example, I was raised by a dad who did the dishes after dinner. Of course Joanne loved this behavior. But I was also raised by parents who were not especially affectionate, so the fact that I picked up some of that behavior required work on my part to overcome my upbringing.

Your significant other will do things that drive you nuts, primarily because those things will be foreign to your understanding of how things should be done. Now, understanding where those behaviors come from may not make them less troublesome to you, but knowing where they come from may at least give you a sense of understanding and maybe even compassion. I know it sounds weird, but think about it. Understanding the root of behavior has two primary benefits: one is to explain the behavior and the second is to address the behavior with a hope of modifying it.

BLANK SLATE BREAKTHROUGHS

Understanding behavior is a primary principle of psychology. We have all heard the saying, "Admitting you have a problem is the first step to getting better." Well, if we don't understand where behavior comes from, it is difficult to acknowledge that it might be a problem. And not admitting a problem makes it impossible to effectively address the problem with a hope of changing it.

Back to Joanne and me. She didn't see clamming up as a

negative behavior. It just was what it was. I saw it as a problem, but until we together discovered the root of the behavior, there was very little chance that we were going to have any effective dialogue about it, or be able to change it. But the same was equally true of me. I didn't see my aggressive communication style as a problem. It was natural to me. Until I was able to acknowledge that that's how I was raised and surrender the idea that my way was the right way, there is no way I would have had the impetus to change.

• • • • • • • • •

My husband's parents divorced when
he was a young teen due to his father's infidelity.
He always says he learned how to be a good
husband and have a good marriage by
NOT doing what his parents did.
I guess it's important to know stuff
like that in the beginning. Sad but true.
—MARLY, COLORADO

• • • • • • • • •

Joanne and I had to look at where we came from or what we were raised with, communicate that to each other, and then start with a blank slate. What does that mean? When we are in a relationship, especially a serious one, we have the opportunity to define how the relationship is going to develop. It is relationally lazy to say, "Hey, this is me. Deal with it." It's not only lazy, but arrogant. What you are saying is that the other person in the relationship is obligated to change to suit your behaviors. Even worse, they might refuse to change too, and you will just bug the heck out of each other for as long as you last (which probably won't be very long).

An important aspect of the "blank slate" is that it needs to be mutually agreed to. It is a sort of contract we enter into with each other in which we say, "I am willing to change if you are." And with that mutual commitment we can begin to experiment with different behaviors that work for the both of us and come up with rules and structures for how we relate.

Another example. When Joanne and I got serious about addressing our communication problem, we created the "time-out rule." When an argument heated up, we would walk away from it (and from each other) for ten minutes. We realized that Joanne needed a little time to think of what she wanted to say and how to say it. And I needed ten minutes to calm down, relax a little, and be ready to come back to the issue with a level head. It worked!

This was probably our first blank slate breakthrough. We decided to create our own rule, our own patterns, and it worked. When we would come back together, we were both more rational and less heated. It redefined the way we interacted and kept us from causing hurt to each other. Over time it became less forced and just began to feel normal. Neither one of us has called for a time-out for years, but the pattern of giving each other space during conflicts remains. It has become as natural as our unhealthy behaviors were in the beginning days of our engagement.

DOING SOME RESEARCH

In your significant relationship you can have your own blank slate breakthrough, but first and foremost, you need to uncover the "why" behind your own behaviors and the behaviors of your significant other. If you don't understand where the behaviors come from, it will be very hard to address them.

Here's what I suggest: Start with yourself. Many of us do things that we ourselves can't understand. We know we have problematic tendencies and preferences, but until we look for the origins of those thoughts and behaviors, it is hard to fix them. So become a self-observer. When you do something that clearly annoys your significant other, or even friends, co-workers, whomever, take a moment to stop and ask yourself, "Why do I do that?" It might take time and soul-searching to figure it out, but believe me, it's worth it. When you realize something about yourself, record your insight in a journal or blog, or just make a simple list. Committing thoughts to paper or your computer makes them real and helps us remember what it is we are trying to figure out, to work on.

It may help to go to the people who know you best to ask them for insight as to why you act a certain way. At this stage in my life, I have Joanne. We have been together for over half our lives, so going to her for help when I am doing something that bothers me or bothers her is a great help. Her insights often help me figure out why I am doing things this way or that. Also, an aunt and uncle of mine have played a huge role in my life. At different times I have gone to them in the process of discovery. At your stage in life, it may be a best friend, a parent, your significant other, your pastor, or a sibling. Whomever you go to, go to them with an open mind and anticipation that you are going to uncover something worth acting on. Discovery of this nature can also be utilized in other parts of your life besides marriage.

OK, so you've entered into this process of self-discovery, but what you really want to know is where your significant other's behaviors come from. There are lots of ways to go about this, but they all start with gaining permission. Your boyfriend or girlfriend isn't going to want you jumping into their past without giving you permission to do that. So ask, "When you shut down in conversation, I really don't understand why that happens. Do you think that's something we could uncover together?" This may be met with resistance, and if it is, you have a pretty clear indication of the teachability and changeability of the person you care about.

I don't want to sound an alarm here, but if you get shut down at this point, you have to be aware that you will be banging your head against this wall for a long time to come. Being in a relationship has the potential to really help us change and grow and improve; but if your other half resists, that's trouble!

But let's assume that you get the go-ahead from this person to begin to search for the origins of a behavior. The place to start is with the person. Some people are very self-aware and will be able to get in touch with where their behavior is coming from. The best way to reveal this is through well-thought-out questions. After all, you don't want to make assumptions; you want to start a good conversation and draw them out in the process.

Another path to discovery is to become an observer. If you have a common group of friends, do you see this behavior manifest itself in relationships other than yours? This should be a big eye-opener for you. If you don't see this behavior arise with others, then the question needs to be asked, "Why does this crop up only with me?"

· · · · · · · · ·

I married someone from a strong Latino
background. It is hard enough to grow together
when you have two people that came from
similar cultures or similar backgrounds.
Then to mix in the fact that we had been raised
in two very different cultures and came from
extremely different backgrounds and family
structures made for a lot of "excitement."

—JASON, CALIFORNIA

· · · · · · · · ·

My favorite way to figure out some of this has been to spend time with Joanne's family. Early in our relationship we both spent a lot of time in each other's homes—we were in high school together and our parents lived less than a mile apart. That experience continues to be invaluable for understanding one another. We were able to see our parents relate to each other, and for better or worse, those are the models we grew up with, the ones we observed and copied to some extent in our own significant relationships.

You may not be in a position to spend much time with your significant other's family, but jump at every chance you get. Not only that, but try to facilitate opportunities for your boyfriend or girlfriend to spend time with *your* family. After all, this is a two-way street. You want them to understand why you do what you do, too. You want them to be able to speak truth into your life that has a basis in observation so that you can continue to mature and develop.

For some couples, "meeting the parents" is something that happens only when the relationship gets very serious or after they become engaged. Big mistake! By that time the stakes are high because of the level of commitment you have already achieved. I have been with couples who have not met or spent time with their significant other's family until they were "past the point of no return" relationally. This happened to some good friends of ours, who met in college and fell in love. But they were thousands of miles away from his family. Her family was a little closer and they would spend time with them on long weekends and on short school holidays. Definitely a plus. But they didn't get time with his family. Can you guess what happened next? When she finally did meet his family and spend a little time with them, she got quite a shock. They were extremely dysfunctional and could barely communicate. This freaked her out (as well it should) because she saw firsthand in his family some of the patterns of behavior that she witnessed in him.

But here's the good part: he was able to recognize the dysfunction in his own family. If he had blown it off or treated it as normal and acceptable, that would have been a serious red flag, as he likely would have brought these patterns into their relationship and would have been resistant to changing them. But when he was around his family with her, he was able to see them through her eyes and was equally shocked.

Today this couple has an amazing relationship. They are self-aware and other-aware, largely because they understand where each other comes from. It is critical in any relationship to know where you come from and where your significant other comes from. There is really no substitute for that. So remember, the best way to get to the root of behaviors is to:

- *Start with you.* You need to be open and willing to be self-aware before you can ask the same of your partner.
- *Ask for permission.* Don't start poking and prodding around their behaviors without asking for permission to do so. Remember, a yes is a good sign and allows you to have confidence in the relationship; a no is a red flag.
- *Become an observer.* It is easier to make assumptions than to become a thoughtful observer, but observation is critical in the process of understanding the "why" behind behavior.
- *Spend time with each other's friends.* You need to get yourself in situations where you can observe your significant other interacting with others. Again, you need permission or an invitation to come into these settings. If your significant other tries to keep you away from their friends, then that's another red flag. To be fair, give your significant other opportunities to meet and interact with your friends.
- *Hang out in each other's homes and with each other's families.* This is the biggest and best way to learn about

your boyfriend or girlfriend. I guarantee that you will learn more about them spending half a day in their home than you could uncover in days' worth of conversation. Once again, you need permission to go there. If they do everything they can to keep you away from their parents, that's trouble.

- *Keep the conversation going.* It would be foolish to think that you'll uncover the issue, discover its source, talk about it, and resolve it just like that. For some of us, the issues that come to the surface are issues that we face throughout much of our lives. Continuing the conversation gives ongoing permission to address the issue.

DISCOVERY QUESTIONS

1. Describe your family. How have your parents provided a model for you, good or bad?

2. If you could change one thing about your family, what would it be?

3. What behavior in your significant other drives you crazy? How do you think they came to have this behavior? If you understood where a troublesome behavior came from, how would it change the way you perceive that behavior?

4. What is a behavior in your own life that you see as completely "normal," but that your significant other sees as a problem? How did your family instill that behavior in you?

5. What is one behavior that you think you need to overcome from how you were brought up?

6. Are you ready to change behaviors that your significant other sees as problems? If you had to rate your significant other's willingness to change on a scale of one to ten, where would they land? What about teachability?

7. What would a "blank slate" look like in your relationship?

8. What spoken or unspoken "rules" do you have in your relationship?

9. If you could create one rule that might help in your relationship, what would it be?

10. Who could you ask for input into behaviors that may be relational stumbling blocks?

11. Have you been around your significant other's family? What was your most important observation?

12. How would you feel about having your significant other spend time around your family? If you are hesitant, why is that?

▶ RED FLAGS

- If you aren't willing to have your significant other search out—with your help—the root of behavior that is causing stress in your relationship, that's a red flag.

- If your significant other puts certain challenging behaviors in the "off-limits" column, that's a red flag.

- If either one of you has significant resistance to spending time with your respective families, that can be a red flag. (There may be good reasons to avoid these interactions, but usually those would be extreme circumstances.)

- Are you observing a behavior, attitude, or issue that you can't talk about? If so, that's a red flag. You have to be willing to bring it up and your significant other has to be willing to discuss it.

CHAPTER 2

Are You Talkin' to Me?
Are You Talkin' to *ME*?

COMMUNICATION

*I truly wish I had known how to communicate
my needs and desires better—emotionally,
spiritually, and physically. I was often a mess and
then I felt I had to "put on the good Christian
wife" face and buck up. So I'd push junky feelings
down and do a slow burn until things just blew!
I truly wish we had invested more time in
learning how to express ourselves.*

—ALLISON, WASHINGTON

Next to family history, the most important building block in a relationship is communication. The simple truth is, if you can't communicate well with your significant other, you're going to have trouble. Communication is the lifeline from which most other relational elements hang.

After Joanne and I were married, we moved to Paris for a few months. Joanne had received an offer to fill in for a woman on maternity leave at a French software company. So a couple of weeks after we graduated, we packed our belongings into a storage facility and moved to Europe. Joanne was a fluent French speaker, having had years and years of French in high school and college. So when we landed in Paris, she was able to communicate just fine, taking care of basic needs like finding an apartment, functioning at her new job, and figuring out where to shop for food.

I had two semesters of French in college. And they were not particularly successful semesters. To be honest, I could barely form a sentence. I would fumble around in my interactions with the clerk at the bakery. I would struggle to figure out what to say to the woman who ran the laundry down the street. Using the local transportation took a while to get used to. It was not an easy time for me.

So why was the transition so easy for Joanne and so the opposite for me? The answer is simple, right? She spent years figuring out how to communicate and I had spent a few months. Do you see the parallel to our discussion of relationships? Some people pay a lot of attention to how they communicate and work hard to improve their communication skills. And some people don't. Just like with any skill—and communication *is* a skill—it takes intentionality and practice to improve. When it came to French, Joanne had both of those, and I had neither.

So, let's move into English. For some people, effective communication comes pretty easily. For most of those people their ease in communication comes from a combination of natural gifting and exposure to effective models of communication. For others, communication is more of a challenge. Sometimes it's because they never witnessed communication modeled effectively, or they are naturally shy or uncomfortable interacting with others. The good news is that for both the gifted communicators and those who struggle, communication is a learned skill and can be improved upon at any stage.

THE COMMUNICATION MODEL

If you have ever taken a communications class, you are probably aware of the basic model for communication. But let's review anyway. It may seem basic, but breaking down communication into its parts may help us understand where breakdowns in communication occur.

First, the "sender" encodes a message and speaks it. Simple, right? That encoding process (deciding what they want to communicate) can happen slowly or lightning fast. Then there is the output of the message. Most of the time this is the spoken word, but sometimes it is a glance, a shrug, or some other form of non-verbal communication.

The context is everything surrounding the message—time, space, atmosphere, emotional temperature, familiarity, and so on. As you well know, the context can play a huge role in how a simple message is communicated and received.

The "receiver" is the recipient of the message. They hear it and then decode it. The message that was carefully—or not so carefully—encoded is rarely received in its purest form: first, because it is passed through the context, and second, because the decoder has their own grid through which the message passes. This grid, in simplest terms, is the receiver's life experience. Whatever we hear passes through everything we know.

So, as you can see, even though most of us have been doing communication our entire lives, there are a number of places where communication can break down. Whether one or both of you struggle with communication, or even if you are both gifted communicators, effective communication is difficult.

The most basic reason for challenges in communication between the two of you is because you have a high level of emotional involvement. You care about each other a great deal, and you may even love each other. In fact, you may be *in love* with each other. Your emotional state significantly drives up the "context" in which your communication occurs. Think about it this way. When you go to a restaurant and order a meal, the communication is pretty easy because there is no emotion involved in the transaction. The waiter wants you to place an order, and you want to place an order, so you transact that business and minutes later your meal shows up.

Change the script a little. Let's say you've been waiting for half an hour and no one at the restaurant has so much as brought you a glass of water. You are getting steamed and when you are just about ready to walk out of the place, your waiter arrives and says, "Whaddaya want?" You are likely to have some emotion involved in your communication that may negatively affect what happens next. The nature of the communication may be different because of the context in which it is occurring.

The strongest emotional context in which to communicate is one of love or deep affection. It colors and clouds everything that passes through it, for better or worse, because when we love someone or when we are *in* love, the communication tends to pass right through our defenses and directly into our heart. You may think that communication between people who love each other, especially romantically, should be easier than it is in other kinds of relationships simply because that affection is there, but honestly, that affection makes communication harder.

IT'S A FAMILY THING

To draw you back to what we talked about in the last chapter, communication is a learned behavior. You and your significant other learned, most likely from immediate family, how to conduct communications. As a result, our communication styles run deep. We have had our communication style ingrained almost from the time we were born.

Changing our communication style won't come easily. Even when communication problems are pointed out to us, we will have a long way to go to effect a change in that style. It takes a long-term and consistent commitment to change to actually accomplish it.

Helping someone change the way they communicate takes a great deal of commitment and patience. Making someone feel like they are under attack will hamper their ability to improve the way they communicate. It is important to speak thoughtfully, carefully, and respectfully when talking to someone about changing communication styles. And you have the right to expect the same.

You need to accept the fact that as foreign as your significant other's communication style seems to you, yours seems just as strange to them. You can't ask someone else to do all the changing. You need to be just as willing to change. If either of you are unwilling or expect the other to do all the changing, this is a big red flag.

SAY WHAT YOU MEAN AND MEAN WHAT YOU SAY

Have you ever heard of a meta message? This is where what is said or done runs contrary to or in addition to the spoken message. Here's an example. When Joanne and I were first married, sometimes Joanne would get upset with something I had done. It was obvious in many ways—mostly nonverbal—that she was upset. I would ask what was wrong and she would reply, "Nothing!" But her expression, tone, and all the other nonverbal clues made it very clear that something was indeed wrong.

This contradictory meta messaging is really damaging in relationships because we want to be able to trust and believe what another person says. If we are convinced that what they say is the opposite of what they mean, it can put us in a position of constantly doubting the truth of what our partner is saying. Obviously that's a problem. So, do you send contradictory meta messages? Does your significant other? If so, you need to talk about it and commit to verbalizing what you really mean.

TALK ABOUT TALKING ABOUT IT

We all have communication preferences. But most of us don't give any thought to what those are. There are ways we like to hear things and ways we like to say things, but have you ever stopped to talk about that with your significant other? Probably not. To start the discussion, become observant. When something is communicated to you that makes you uncomfortable, make a mental note of it. Often, the timing isn't right for you to address it on the spot and that's OK. Just remember that you need to talk about it later.

• • • • • • • • • •

One of the major adjustments for us was that we had both lived our whole lives making our own decisions. All of a sudden, before making a decision, we had to consult our spouse; we had to communicate about every little thing, from what color to paint the bedroom to mayonnaise or Miracle Whip. In most cases, it wasn't anything big, but just adding that second layer of communication and approval to a lot of our decisions made it rough in the beginning.

—Martha, Indiana

• • • • • • • • •

An example might be that your significant other has a very didactic communication style, meaning they make matter-of-fact statements that leave very little opportunity for response. Something like—"It's cold outside. You should have worn a different outfit." OK, that's very direct and to the point, but it may also sound a little combative. Nothing wrong with what was communicated here, but the style may get on your nerves.

You could tuck this away and come back to it. If you address it in the moment, chances are it won't be received well. So, later on you can say something like, "You know, when you commented on my outfit it was a little abrupt. Maybe in the future you could ask a question or make a suggestion when you have something like that to communicate." And you have to expect that your partner will have similar communication-style input for you as you grow closer.

So here's the thing: if either or both of you are resistant to this sort of feedback, that's a problem. Everyone has their own "language." It is up to us to learn the language of our significant other, and our partner needs to learn ours. That makes total sense, right? So if you or your significant other are resistant to learning it, red flag!

This certainly isn't an easy process, and that's where lots of us get tripped up. After all, we want communication with this special someone to be fun and easy and all that other good stuff. But because we care for them, maybe even love them, it will be easier for us to hurt them. And we are more susceptible to being hurt by this communication too. Your emotions are going to be closer to the surface, so mutually agree that you are going to learn each other's language and take it gently.

Let's review:

- Learning to communicate with your significant other can be a little like learning to speak a foreign language. It is going to take time and you are going to make a few mistakes along the way.

- Communication involves more than just words. It includes context and all sorts of nonverbal cues. As important as it is to pay attention to what we say, we need to be attentive to other variables like time, place, tone, and intent, as well.

- Meta messaging can erode trust in a relationship. After all, if I can't believe what you say, I will end up second-guessing you all the time.

- Be aware that this process is a lot of work. But remember that it is the basis for everything else that happens in a relationship. If your communication is poor, there is very little chance that other aspects of your relationship will be able to withstand this weakness. So give it the attention it deserves and talk about how to talk!

DISCOVERY QUESTIONS

1. Rate your communication with your significant other on a scale of one to ten. Where does it fall? Why?

2. Have you ever intentionally worked to improve the way you communicate? If so, what was the primary area of your focus?

3. What is your primary stumbling block to good communication?

4. What other factors would you add to this model of communication (sender, context, receiver)?

5. What are your top five rules for effective communication? List them in order of importance.

6. Do you find that communicating with someone you love is

significantly more challenging than communicating with someone you care about less? Why do you think that is?

7. What is your most ingrained communication behavior? Why is it so deeply seated?

8. If your significant other pointed out your deeply seated communication behaviors, how would you react? How do you think your significant other would react if you brought up one of their communication behaviors?

9. Are you willing to make substantial changes to your communication style for the sake of your relationship? Is your significant other willing to change?

10. What meta messages do you send? Why do you think you do that?

11. What meta messages does your significant other send? How do you react or respond to those messages?

12. Can you think of a time when you and your significant other were able to address a communication issue well? How about one that you addressed poorly?

▶ RED FLAGS

- If you rated your communication with your significant other a five or below, that's a red flag. You can overcome a low score but you have to be prepared to do a lot of work.

- If one or both of you has a problem with meta messages, that's a considerable challenge for you to overcome. It's doable, but you need to be prepared for some real work in this area.

- If you or your significant other see the communication

problems in the relationship as solely the problem of the other, that's a red flag. Communication is a two-way street and the breakdown in communication is rarely a one-sided problem.

- Are you observing communication breakdowns in your significant other's relationships? If so, chances are the same will occur in your own relationship. If you two can talk about it, that's a plus. But if you can't discuss it? Red flag.

●

CHAPTER 3

Do You Fight Dirty?

CONFLICT RESOLUTION

*I thought we wouldn't fight! We really didn't
have arguments when we were dating so I wasn't
prepared for the fights that came after we were
married. It was really hard to do it without
hurting each other—at least I felt hurt a lot.*

—Mindy, Montana

The best time to talk about how you manage conflict, or how you argue with one another, is *not* during an argument! Every couple is going to fight from time to time, and learning how to do it effectively and with the least damage possible is key to a healthy, sustainable relationship. But you have to get ahead of the game and talk about how to fight fairly when you aren't fighting. I know, it doesn't sound like fun to spend your time together talking about that subject, but believe me, it will pay off.

Joanne and I had our first real knock-down, drag-out fight over towels. When we were first married and moving into our new apartment, we were unpacking boxes. I put the linens in the linen closet, which involved folding all the towels. After I was done I moved on to another project, but I noticed that Joanne was taking out all the towels and refolding them the wrong way. And I told her so. I proceeded to move her out of the way and set about refolding the refolded towels the right way. That's when things went south in a hurry. I think the argument ended with Joanne locking herself in the bathroom.

When we look back at the conflict it is now easy to see that we fought the way we had been trained to fight in our families. I had been taught to be aggressive and Joanne had been taught to retreat. These two tendencies blended like oil and water. I came on like a ton of bricks and Joanne got out of there fast. At that point in our relationship the other's behavior made no sense. I expected her to fight back. Maybe she expected that I'd be like her dad and just step in and make the final decision. Or maybe she expected me to withdraw too. Of course that didn't happen.

The argument stopped being about the towels and started to be about us hurting each other. The natural tendency is to cut each other when we get into a fight. Think about your last conflict. Chances are that what ended up hurting you the most wasn't the fact that you disagreed about something, but that in the process of disagreeing, cutting remarks were made. And when that happens, we respond out of our pain. Things are bound to get ugly.

We both wanted to win, regardless of the cost. Even people who are noncompetitive by nature have a drive to be right. That's human nature. So when the emotional temperature goes up, we get determined, we dig in, and we decide—often in a split second or on a subconscious level—that we are going to win this one! This is a destructive impulse, and difficult to deal with. And of course the source of this behavior is a self-convinced sense of our own rightness. This mind-set causes us to strive to win, and in the process we are perfectly happy to make someone else lose.

We forget that the person we are fighting with is someone we care about, sometimes very, very much. For whatever reason, when the emotional temperature rises on an argument, the care and affection we may have for the person we're arguing with flies right out the window. In fact, it is largely because of these strong feelings for our significant other that the emotional temperature rises so quickly. As hard as it can be to do this, we each need to take a moment to remember how we really feel about the person we are battling against. In many situations, reminding each other of the care we have for one another can ratchet down the conflict.

IT'S HUMAN NATURE

Have you ever spent time around toddlers? At a very young age, they learn how to fight with each other. One of the first words kids learn to say is "mine." That's human nature at work. No one sets out to teach a little kid to say "mine" but they learn it anyhow. And the root of that is that kids want what they want—they are willful and selfish. But of course as adults we grow out of that, right? If only that were the case. Maybe we get better about it—we don't put our toys in a death grip and scream "MINE!"—but we like having our way and will fight to have it just so. It's in our nature.

So how does that affect how we fight? The short answer is, most fights are about having our own way. And with that goal in mind, we are denying what the person on the other end of the fight wants. Think about it. I bet you can draw a line from each of your recent fights back to this very principle.

AND, WE'VE BEEN TRAINED THAT WAY

It's human nature to be selfish, but, in addition, we are often exposed to models that are unhealthy and unhelpful. The models of conflict in my own life have been less than perfect—although some are better than others. One model is out-and-out war: both parties dig in and won't relinquish any ground. In another model, both parties become passive-aggressive and end up sulking. A third model allows one person always to claim to be right and the other to always expect that they are wrong. Sounds pretty lame, huh? None of these are models I want to emulate.

But in times of stress we go with what we know. When life gets difficult, our rational brain shuts down and our instinctive brain takes over. So we revert to the models we have been exposed to, whether we like them or not. This is often where the damage gets done. Sounds pretty grim, right? The point is, we have to relearn conflict behavior. We have to share our models with our significant other and ask them to do the same so that when we revert to negative or destructive behavior in conflict, we can call it out, set it aside, and try to do it the right way. This isn't easy and may take a lot of time and commitment to learn how to do well, but if you won't do it, you are in for a world of hurt.

PRINCIPLE 1: MAKE SURE YOU KNOW WHAT YOU'RE FIGHTING ABOUT

This brings up our first principle: make sure you know what you are really fighting about. Just like with the meta messaging we talked about, it is easy to think you are fighting about one subject while your partner thinks you are arguing about something completely different. Typically this happens because there is a trigger that sets off conflict but the trigger itself become secondary as the fight becomes more personal and increasingly more painful. So it's not a bad idea, when you feel the conflict start to rise up, to pause and clarify what you are discussing. Remember, when arguments escalate, it often becomes less about the trigger and more about the damage that is being done in the context of the argument.

Joanne and I may have been irked by each other's approach to folding towels, and I think either one of us would have been smart enough to know that it wasn't something worth fighting about, but when the conflict started, words were said that triggered a much more significant reaction. That escalation is what we want to avoid. So when you find yourself in conflict it is good to take a minute to clarify, "OK, let me make sure I know what we're really disagreeing about here." Sometimes just doing this will eliminate a lot of the conflict because stating it will take the sting out of it. You may realize that what you're battling over just isn't worth it.

PRINCIPLE 2: STICK TO THE TOPIC AT HAND

Second, besides naming the thing you're fighting about, it is important to stick to the topic at hand. Sometimes in conflict it's easy to bring up all sorts of past and potentially unresolved issues, turning the fight into a grab bag of grievances. This is a huge no-no. Most of us have seen this happen, usually in an attempt to put one or the other of you in your place by bringing up a hurt or wrong that has been long gone, and it can be ugly.

For example, Joanne and I had a big fight in college after we were engaged. The argument came to a head in front of the dining hall on our campus, and in front of a number of other students. In the heat of the argument Joanne ripped off her engagement ring, threw it at me, and stormed off. That was painful (not that I didn't deserve it). In the following weeks and even months, it would have been very easy for me to draw on that incident as a way of beating Joanne down. Something like, "You're criticizing me? You're the one who threw your ring at me and stormed off in front of all those people!"

If I had done that, only two things could have been accomplished. First, I would have intentionally inflicted pain on Joanne. Obviously this situation became as embarrassing to her as it was to me. By bringing it up, I would be looking to take her down a notch and cause her to feel badly about herself.

Second, I may have been able to silence her. Sometimes we go to this "nuclear" option because we think the impact of bringing up a past hurt will be so significant that it will blow the current disagreement out of the water altogether.

So you have to agree together that you simply won't do that. There is a time and a place to bring up past hurts as a means of processing through and resolving them; in fact, this is critical to a healthy relationship—no one wants to walk around with a bag of past hurts over their shoulder. But opening up that bag during unrelated conflict is nothing but bad news. So agree with each other that you simply won't do it.

In the heat of battle, even if you have come to that agreement, it still may happen. If it does, the situation requires a time-out to say, "Hey, this isn't the time or place to get into a past hurt. Let's stick to the topic." It's also a good idea to pay attention when a past hurt is inappropriately brought up because it is likely something unresolved that needs to be addressed at a later time.

PRINCIPLE 3: REACH A WIN–WIN COMPROMISE

Third, you and your significant other need to reach a win-win compromise. This is a tough one because it runs against our natural bent and is totally countercultural. When we get in a conflict, something is triggered within us, compelling us to win. At any cost. Come out on top. Be vindicated. And especially, we want the fact that we felt the need to escalate this situation into an argument to be justified.

If we are working toward a win, we often feel like what we say and do to get to that win is justified. But this natural tendency is a relationship killer. When someone wins and someone loses, that creates a power imbalance.

Now I know it sounds weird that there would be a power dynamic in a romantic relationship, but the reality is that all relationships have some form of power balance. In your job, for instance, your boss has some power because the boss is the chief determinant as to whether you get to keep the job. But you have power in that relationship too because you are a critical part of getting the work done. You also have some power because you have the choice to leave whenever you want. Now most of the time the balance of power in a dating relationship is pretty balanced—you are both in it together with the same opportunities to stay or go. But think about the relationships you have seen where one person is more in love than the other. In that sort of a relationship the one who loves more is usually willing to take being treated poorly for the sake of staying in the relationship. And the one who loves less usually realizes the imbalance and may take advantage of it, treating the other shabbily. After all, they can get away with it.

· · · · · · · · ·

Getting in disagreements after we were married was totally different than when we were dating because now it was permanent and whatever it took we were going to have to work it out. Most of the time I would just want to leave the house or something, but I knew I was going to be coming back to the same thing, so I might as well stay and try to work it out.

—MARK, ARIZONA

· · · · · · · · ·

So, when someone wins and someone loses, that can create a power imbalance. After all, when someone loses, they are a loser. That's a lousy position to be in. What we really want is for both parties to win. So how do you do that? The answer is simple: you need to work it out, as best you can, to your mutual satisfaction. But the practice of it is challenging.

Let's go back to the towel crisis from earlier in this chapter. Both Joanne and I were convinced that we had folded the towels correctly. Both of us were convinced that the other had folded the towels wrong. We battled to see who would be right, who would win. The better solution would have been to explain that the way we folded them was the way we had been taught to fold. No big deal, and we could have decided together what way we were going to fold towels in our new married relationship. Pretty simple.

But towels weren't really the issue, were they? The bigger issue was that each of us felt inconvenienced—that's what the fight was really about. So the win-win solution there would have been for us to put a name to the real reason behind our fight. And once we had done that, my guess is that we would have realized that arguing over inconvenience was pretty silly and we could have moved on. But that didn't happen because we both wanted to win.

The point is, always work for the win-win. If you don't, then someone in the relationship will become a loser. And if you really care for someone, you never want to see that happen. In fact, if you are in a relationship with someone who is happy to see you lose an argument, then that's a red flag.

PRINCIPLE 4: REMEMBER YOU LOVE EACH OTHER

Finally, remember you love each other. This one seems almost too simple, but it is maybe the most profound of the principles when dealing with conflict. The reason it's so important is because it is so easy to forget but so key for resolving conflict. Admit it, when you really get into it with your significant other, the fact that you love him or her, or at least really care for him or her, goes right out the window. What you feel during these heightened emotional times is probably anything but love.

That's why in the middle of conflict it is important to take a breath, step back, and remind yourself of a couple of things. Remind yourself why you are in this relationship in the first place. Now, to be fair, if you only give it a minute's thought, you may not come up with anything. It happens! All of us have been in the position of thinking, "What am I doing here?" But that is a temporary feeling and chances are it's going to pass. If it doesn't, or if you find yourself spending a lot of time thinking, why am I in this relationship? then it may be time to bail out. If you can't answer that question, especially if you're asking yourself as a result of constant conflict, then, you guessed it—red flag.

As counterintuitive as it seems, when you are in the middle of conflict it might be a good idea to affirm the feelings you have for each other that have kept you together to this point. I know, it sounds weird. But if you can take a breath and let someone know, regardless of what's going on in the moment, that you really do care for them, that you want them to win, and that you know this is just a temporary thing, it will do wonders in bringing down the emotional temperature of an argument. After all, when was the last time someone paused and told you how much they cared about you in the middle of a dispute? It just doesn't happen, but when it does, it can be powerful.

So be prepared to "mix it up" sometimes. After all, disagreements happen in every relationship. But make sure you do it right. The right kind of argument will help to resolve your conflict and will have you both walking away feeling positive.

DISCOVERY QUESTIONS

1. What was the last argument you had with your significant other? What was the best thing about your argument? Can you think of anything good that came from it?

2. What's the dumbest thing you and your significant other have ever fought about (e.g., towels)? Can you identify what the fight was *really* about (e.g., inconvenience)?

3. What models of conflict have you been exposed to? For better or worse, what models have you had for how to deal with conflict? How have they affected the way you argue or deal with conflict?

4. What is one behavior in conflict that you wish you could change in yourself? What is one that you wish your significant other would change?

5. In an argument with your significant other, have you ever intentionally tried to cause damage apart from the topic of the argument? What happened as a result?

6. Have you been in an argument only to discover that the two of you weren't fighting about the same thing? How did you figure that out?

7. Have you ever had your significant other use something from your past against you? How did that feel?

8. In your desire to win an argument, what other techniques do you use to "silence" your significant other?

9. Have you ever won an argument only to find that the victory felt hollow? Why do you think that was?

10. What do you think about this idea of "power dynamic" in your dating relationship? What is the balance of power in your relationship?

11. Have you ever been able to achieve a win-win in an argument with your significant other? If not, what do you think it would take to make that happen in your next argument?

12. What do you think would happen if you stopped in the middle of a conflict and took the time to tell each other how you really feel about one another, not at that very moment, but in the big picture of things?

RED FLAGS

The reality is, if you are in any sort of romantic relationship, there is going to be conflict—maybe not at first but over time, it's going to happen. So, it's important at every stage of the relationship to look for red flags and address them as soon as possible. Don't be freaked out if some of these red flags pop up—they do in every relationship and they often can be worked through. However, if your significant other won't acknowledge these conflict-related problems or isn't willing to address them with you, then you have a problem.

- You need to know why you handle conflict the way you do, which means you need to be able to look at your family history and other significant experiences to explain why you do what you do. This will help your partner understand your tendencies and will give them more patience when conflict arrives. Your significant other needs to be willing to do the same. If they can't or won't, that's a red flag. If they are not willing or able to talk about how they came to manage conflict the way they do, then it doesn't give you much of a chance to work together to reshape your collective approach to conflict.

- Don't go to the past to bring up old hurts in order to win an argument. You need to stick to the topic at hand. If your partner refuses to play by the rules and constantly brings up old hurts and faults in an attempt to hurt you or silence you, then that's a red flag.

- Make sure you know what you're fighting about. Sometimes the fight isn't about what it seems to be about. It is absolutely critical to make sure you both are fighting about the same issue. He may think you are arguing about how you drive his car; she may think you're arguing about how you yelled at her and made her feel attacked. So sort it out. A lot of times doing this resolves some, if not all, of the conflict. Unwillingness to do so is a red flag.

- Go for the win-win. It's not about one person winning and one person losing. If you can't work together to ensure that the argument is worked out to the satisfaction of both sides, then that's a red flag.

- If you can't honestly say that you still care for or even

love each other in the midst of a conflict, that's a problem. Your care for each other shouldn't be so fragile as to rise and fall simply because of a conflict. If you or your partner lose sight of that during conflict, that's a red flag.

•

CHAPTER 4

Do You Take Plastic?

MONEY AND FINANCES

Financially, I wish I had been better prepared
for what it would be like to pay all the bills—my
parents had been paying for everything. Little did
I know that quite a few of the dates and gifts and
even the engagement ring were still on credit cards.
So when we married, we began in debt. That has
been a struggle for us all of our almost seventeen
years (but we are getting better at communicating
about finances with the Lord's help!).

—JENNA, MISSOURI

Did you know that more marriages end over money issues than almost any other issue? So that is reason enough for us to talk about how you and your significant other view money, spend money, and save money. At this point in your relationship, you haven't combined your finances, but if you continue on, the day will come when what's yours will mingle with what's his or hers. And if you don't have a good sense of what that will entail and how it will affect you, it's time to start asking some questions and looking for red flags.

First, a story: Joanne and I grew up about a quarter of a mile from each other. Our families had similar houses, similar cars, took similar vacations, and seemed to have similar spending patterns. However, there was one key difference that didn't come to light until after we were married. Joanne's family was a cash-only family. With the exception of their mortgage, they never borrowed money for anything. They paid cash for their cars, clothes, and vacations.

My family was a little different. My parents were more likely to use credit cards to pay for purchases and then try to pay off the balances over time. In the process, they racked up some debt that affected them down the road. But when I lived at home, seeing them pull out the Visa was pretty normal. What this meant is that Joanne grew up ingrained with little or no tolerance for being in debt and I grew up quite comfortable with it. Because we were both young and impressionable, what our parents did seemed normal to us. What we didn't think about is how abnormal our family's behaviors would seem to the other.

HOW YOU SPEND

What is your personal strategy with money? Are you cash-only or do you buy on credit? It's really a bigger deal than it may appear. If you are used to spending on credit and your partner isn't, and if somewhere down the road you plan to get married and combine finances, then they inherit your debt. Many couples get together expecting that they have similar views on debt. The partner who has worked very hard to stay out of debt or to minimize their use of credit all of a sudden may find themselves knee-deep, thousands of dollars in debt, and believe me, that has significant impact on their future.

· · · · · · · · ·

Financial issues have been and still are a struggle in our home. I would say that I still haven't accepted responsibility for this area of our lives, and I'm afraid my wife suffers for it.

—BRIAN, CALIFORNIA

· · · · · · · · ·

Friends of mine fell in love at law school. They had a great dating relationship and got married. So far so good. However, they both brought their student loan debt to the marriage—what ended up being tens of thousands of dollars. They had a monthly obligation of thousands of dollars. So what did this mean to them? While their friends were buying houses, they were servicing their debt. While their friends were buying new cars, they were making loan payments. The amount of debt they had put them back years in terms of activities that you would expect a newly married couple to engage in.

The good news is that they are still happily married. They have two beautiful kids, they have been able to buy a house, and they have two decent cars. The only difference is that it took them years and years to be able to afford these things. Let's be clear: the fact that they had student loans isn't bad. If you are going to go into debt, this is a pretty good reason. But it did mean that their life was very different from their peers. And they knew what they were getting into. Because they both had loans, they were "equally yoked" in terms of debt and it didn't breed resentment between them.

Now imagine if only one of them brought this debt to the party. Can you imagine the potential for conflict that might have arisen as a result? It is one thing if you are both in it together. It is another if you feel like you have been saddled or burdened with someone else's debt that is keeping you from the life or lifestyle you envisioned.

This is something that is good and right to talk about when a relationship starts to get serious. And really, simple observation will give you a sense of how debt and credit use is viewed. Do you reach for the credit card every time you go shopping together? Does your partner reach for the plastic every time you are out to dinner? Either way, you need to talk about it. If your significant other is unwilling to talk about credit use and debt, that's a red flag. If either of you has a mountain of debt—or if you both do— then as a couple you are going to have to wrestle through what that means for your relationship. After all, for many, the debt that is incurred in early adulthood will stick around for years.

HOW YOU LIVE

How you live may sound like an unusual topic, but you need to have this discussion. Joanne and I never talked about this one before we got married and it caused all sorts of trouble for us after we tied the knot. We each just assumed we would live the way our families lived. We assumed we would live somewhere nice, drive a relatively new car, take nice vacations, eat out, and shop for clothes at Nordstrom. That's what we were used to and that's how things were in our families. Can you guess the problem?

We got married during Christmas break of our junior year in college. We both had jobs and made enough money to cover our expenses if we lived frugally, but that was about it. But in our minds there was no reason not to live the lifestyle that we were accustomed to, even though our income couldn't support it. So we lived the high life on credit. We never once had the conversation about the fact that maybe we needed to dial it back a little because our income was so small. I don't think it even crossed our minds.

So we lived on credit cards and loans. Vacations, a new car, lots of meals out, and a great wardrobe. We also racked up almost twenty thousand dollars of debt after only a few years of marriage. You see, we didn't talk about how we wanted to live so we just assumed a lifestyle that we couldn't really support. If we had sat down and really talked it through, I think we would have made some different decisions.

So what does this mean for you? First off, you need to pay attention to the lifestyle that you live today and likewise for your significant other. Do you live within your means or do you use credit to support your lifestyle? Do you drive a new car every couple of years or are you happy to drive the one you have into the ground? What about your levels of consumption? Do you shop a lot, or does your significant other? Do you eat out all the time? All of these are important questions to ask yourself and to talk about with your partner.

As things get more serious, you have to come to a joint understanding of how you are going to live. You can see that this is a multifaceted issue. It has a lot to do with how each of you were raised. It has a lot to do with how you view debt. So addressing this issue will actually bring to the surface a couple of others. But it is a conversation or two—or ten—that needs to happen if someday you are going to comingle your finances.

You can see where problems might arise, right? Imagine that you are very frugal and are happy with a simple life not driven by accumulation. Now imagine your significant other is a really, really active consumer. The opportunity for conflict is plain. But it is nothing that you can't get ahead of through intentional conversations and a willingness to change. It may also be time to talk budgets.

The easiest way to see if there is a discrepancy in the lifestyle department is to work on your budget and to have your significant other do the same. Obviously this isn't something to do on a first date, but it can be an interesting exercise. It will be pretty easy to see where their priorities lie when you see how they arrange their finances on paper. And you might learn a thing or two about your own habits when you write it down. But here is the bigger issue. Do you and your partner stick to your budgets? Lots of married couples have a budget written down somewhere that they never follow; it is more of an ideal than a reality. So that's another question to ask.

Just be aware. If your significant other uses credit and is amassing debt to pay for their lifestyle, then that debt is going to come with them into whatever future relationship they have. And nothing creates conflict or affects future lifestyle like a ton of debt. It will affect your ability to buy a home, it will affect your ability to get loans, and it will mean that potentially a significant portion of your income will go toward debt service. So if you or your partner is living high on the hog through credit, be prepared for some hard conversations and even harder choices.

Now for the red flags. If you and your partner have polar views on lifestyle, then you're facing a challenge that can take a lot of effort to work out. If you are both convinced that your way is the right way and don't see merit in the other way, then that's a red flag. Obviously, you won't have this discussion early in a relationship, but as things get serious it's necessary to talk about it. An unwillingness to discuss these issues is another red flag.

Keep in mind that lifestyle may be one of the most important conversations that you will have as a potentially engaged couple, so don't shortchange it or gloss over it.

HOW YOU SAVE AND GIVE

Just as important as how you spend your money is how you save it and give it away. Differences in this philosophy can cause real trouble in a relationship if this ground isn't well covered and your giving plan mutually agreed to.

Joanne and I never talked about how we were going to spend. And having not cleared that hurdle we never talked about saving or giving money away. I think we both had an idea that saving was beneficial. And we had both grown up with some under-standing of the importance of giving a portion of your income away to a church or other Christian organization. But we never talked about it. As a result, Joanne and I both had a growing sense of dissatisfaction with how we were dealing with our money. Believe it or not, the fact that we weren't saving and giving made us even more discontent with how we were locked into a pattern of debt reduction and consumerism that kept us from doing the right thing.

· · · · · · · · ·

I wish I would have known how much
saving early on would impact our lives later.
We are seeing some things that could have been
avoided had we thought ahead three years
to having kids and one income.
—Heidi, South Carolina

· · · · · · · · ·

Now the challenge for us was that we didn't get off on the right foot. We didn't start out with an understanding or agreement that we would give and save. In subtle ways our dissatisfaction with how we were treating money turned into resentment between us. It is easy to look at your significant other and see them as a barrier to what you want or what you think is right. That happened to us. It didn't result in big talks or fights or anything like that, just an underlying concern that stuck with us.

If we had talked before we were engaged about how we were going to save and give, and if we had continued that conversation into our marriage, we would have had a strong foundation for living out what we thought was important instead of letting our circumstances dictate our actions.

After we were married, Joanne and I decided that before we had a baby we would do two things: own a home and have no credit card debt. Well, when Joanne got pregnant we did own a townhouse, but we still had about nine thousand dollars in credit card debt. I was particularly concerned that we were bringing a baby into the world while we were still so deep in the hole. And my concern was made even more acute by the fact that we wanted the option for Joanne to be a stay-at-home mom. With our debt load there was just no way to make that happen. So I sought the advice of a good friend. His words changed our thinking on giving. He told me that if I wanted to get out of debt I should first of all pray that God would help us get out of our debt, and then increase our giving.

Now both pieces of advice seemed counterintuitive. First off, I felt like we had gotten ourselves into this debt and that getting out was all about us working it off. I honestly didn't see what God had to do with it, and I even felt like God was disappointed with how we had gotten ourselves into this position and we needed to get out of it to be right with him.

Furthermore, every extra penny was going to the credit card company, so how in the world were we supposed to increase our giving? But in my friend's words, what did we have to lose? We started to pray and we started to give. And the next nine months brought amazing results. Checks showed up in the mail that we didn't expect. I got a raise and a couple bonuses at work. And wouldn't you know it, the week after Audrey was born we sent our last payment in to the credit card company.

Now I am not a name-it-and-claim-it prosperity gospel guy. But I do believe passionately that God is concerned with our financial life and that he cares about how we spend, save, and give. I also believe that he wants us to keep him in the loop when it comes to these decisions. I believe he wants us to pray over big spending decisions and that he desires us to acknowledge that all our material wealth comes from him.

DISCOVERY QUESTIONS

1. Can you explain fairly concisely how your family viewed money when you were growing up? Can you concisely explain your own views on money?

2. What kind of debt are you bringing to the relationship? How do you think your significant other would feel if all of a sudden your debt became their debt?

3. What kind of debt might your significant other bring to the relationship? Are you comfortable with that debt level?

4. Do you currently have the income to support your lifestyle? Does your significant other?

5. Have you ever taken the time to talk about what your future together might look like in terms of lifestyle? Does it mesh with what you think you will be able to support if you combine finances?

6. Do you and your significant other currently share a similar lifestyle? How are your lifestyles similar or different?

7. Do you currently have a budget? Would you be willing to share it with your significant other?

8. Do you currently save and/or give money to your church or other Christian organization? Does your significant other?

9. If you were to step up your giving, how do you think that would affect your overall view of money?

⚑ RED FLAGS

So, how do you feel about finances? What does your significant other think about money? I can tell you firsthand that if you aren't on the same page or if you aren't talking about it, you are in red flag territory. Think about it like this: your balance of spending, saving, and giving is a barometer to your financial health. Keeping them in a balance you mutually agree on prevents finances from becoming a source of strife between you and your significant other if you move toward making your relationship permanent. Here are some other red flags:

- If your lifestyle is completely different than your significant other's in terms of spending, saving, and giving, you are going to have an uphill battle if you decide to take the next steps in your relationship. You can overcome different financial backgrounds and habits, but only if the two of you are willing to honestly discuss finances and make changes. If you can't talk about it, that's a big red flag.

- If you or your partner has a ton of debt, little income, and no real plan or strategy for eliminating that debt, this is going to cause significant strife if the relationship moves forward. It's not a deal breaker, but you need to be open and honest about where you are financially, and you need to expect the same from your significant other. If you can't bring yourself to disclose, or if your significant other can't let you in to this aspect of their life, that's a red flag.

- If you are a big believer in saving and giving, and your significant other doesn't think it's that big a deal, that will create problems if you merge finances. You need to talk about why it's important or unimportant to embrace these activities. Again, being on opposite sides of these issues is going to really get you later. Red flag.

- Being on completely different pages financially may not be a deal breaker if you are in love and intend to spend the rest of your lives together, but statistics show that millions of marriages end every year over money. Simple as that. So don't assume that your love for each other is going to render insignificant the differences you have over money and what to do with it. If you think it's no big deal and that it'll sort itself out in the end, that's a massive red flag.

•

CHAPTER 5

Why Aren't Your Friends Normal?

FRIENDSHIPS AND COMMUNITY

Spend less time with your individual friends and
more with your spouse, and never embarrass your
spouse in public (even if you are joking).

—JONATHAN, MARYLAND

We can't make it through this life without friends. And even if we could, why would we want to? Friends add a richness and a sense of community and belonging to our lives. If you are in a serious dating relationship, you have probably already thought about friends and the bigger role they play not only in your life, but in the life of your significant other. Just like families merge when you tie the knot, your friendships and sense of community also merge. His friends aren't going anywhere if you take things to the next level, and her friends are going to be her friends no matter what the change in the status of your relationship. So you'd better be talking about those relationships, what they mean for you, and what your expectations are relating to them.

YOURS, MINE, AND OURS

We need our friends. It's not that they are nice accessories, it's that they are there to perform an important role in our lives. Now if you are in a significant relationship, you have undoubtedly seen changes in the nature of those friendships. The first and most obvious probably being that you don't have the same amount of discretionary time to dedicate to them. That's OK. Everyone expects that when you are in a serious relationship, your time is going to be reallocated.

But don't fall into the trap of thinking that your significant other is all you need, and devalue the rest of your friendships as a result. That would be a big mistake. As much as we might like to believe it's true, our significant other can't meet all of our relational needs. Hear me out. We'd like to think that everything we need in terms of relationship and community can be taken care of in our most significant relationship, but the immense strain that would put on a relationship is usually more than it can bear.

When Joanne and I were married in college, we intentionally kept up our existing friendships. We had seen a number of couples on campus get married and then disappear. They no longer participated in campus life and they walked away from a lot of their friends and the communities that they had been involved in. Don't get me wrong, there is a time to cocoon after you take that big step in your relationship—after all, you are in love and desire to be intimate with your spouse—but you have to hold that in balance with the fact that you still need other people, and especially community, if you are going to make the relationship work in the long run.

For example, after Joanne and I got serious with each other, I also got serious about golf. My freshman year of college, an uncle gave me a set of clubs and Joanne's dad took me out to the driving range a couple of times and then out onto the course. I loved golf right from the start. Joanne didn't. Goodness knows that she tried to like it. She would come along on some of these golf outings, but she just couldn't get into it. Enter my friend Trent. Trent was a good friend and a really good golfer, and we started playing golf together a couple times a week. I have incredibly fond memories of afternoons spent on the course with Trent and I wouldn't want to trade them.

If I didn't have a close relationship with Trent and if I expected Joanne to be my golfing buddy, one of two things would have happened: either I would have given up golf, or I would have forced Joanne into an activity she didn't enjoy in the least. Both of these options are bad. I have seen both scenarios happen for many couples, and it's always to the long-term detriment of their relationship.

This is a simple illustration and the reality is that if I had had to give up golf and, moreover, my good golfing buddy Trent, in order to honor my relationship with Joanne, I could have done it. But making these sacrifices might have planted seeds of resentment in the process. Think about your own friendships. What would happen if your significant other asked you to give up one or two of your closest ones? What result might that produce in your life? What would that tell you about the nature of your relationship? These are important questions to ask.

I CAN'T STAND SO-AND-SO!

We all have that friend who is loveable to us and is a complete pain in the neck to everyone else. I'm not sure why God gives us these strange relationships but he does. I have had a friend or two, especially in college, who were really off the charts in terms of their ability to annoy people, including Joanne. So, what to do? Do I drop a friend just because Joanne finds him annoying? Probably not. There are a couple things to do in order to keep a relationship intact when your significant other objects.

First, you need to be able to express what it is you value about your friend. Sometimes providing context to the relationship and being able to explain why the relationship is significant to you can help your significant other see someone through another lens and might even get them to appreciate that friendship for what it is.

Second, accept that this friendship may not become a friendship between your friend and your significant other, and that you may need to let that expectation go by the wayside. It is natural to want our friends to also be friends with the most significant person in our lives, but it is really OK if they aren't accepting of each other. Being OK with their distance is a big part of keeping both relationships healthy.

But here is a caveat. Some people in our lives may not be good for us. Our significant other knows us and loves us and wants the best for us. In that role, they have an obligation to point out things in our lives that may be unhealthy or detrimental. And that may extend to a friendship or two. This is a tough one and needs to be handled with the utmost care.

You don't want to create a them-or-me situation. I have seen couples where she has said, "You have to choose. Is it going to be your friend, or are you going to choose me?" Wow—what a mistake! If you are looking to breed resentment in your relationship, this is a great way to do it. In these situations you have to be gentle, careful, and thoughtful.

You can't start the conversation about the friend with, "I can't stand so-and-so!" That's really not the point. We all have friends who are uniquely ours and who aren't necessarily among our significant other's favorite people. That's OK. What you need to do is start out by asking questions about why this particular relationship is important. When you uncover this, you will be more compassionate as you proceed. Very carefully, you need to be able to point out specific ways in which you think the relationship might be detrimental or unhealthy. Don't speak in generalities, as they can be easily dismissed. And make sure you speak the truth in love. It is easy in these situations to do one without the other.

At the end of the day, the person your significant other values may not go by the wayside, even at your request. So you have a decision to make. Is that relationship so destructive that it will prevent the two of you from growing closer? If so, that's a red flag. Is the relationship causing destructive behavior like drug use, alcohol abuse, gambling, profanity, or other ungodly behavior? Then you have to be willing to have a tough conversation that may lead to you making a change. These are tough situations so don't expect them to be straightforward or easy. Chances are it will be anything but. If your significant other isn't willing to at least discuss their friendships, if they are unable to see the negative effects of a friendship on their lives, and if they become defensive or combative when you bring it up, these are troublesome red flags.

• • • • • • • • •

My dad sat both of us down (separately)
and talked to us about the need to be each
other's best friend—my hubby over the
girlfriends, and me to my hubby over the guys.
He told us about how it took him years to
understand that and that there were things early
on that he shared "with the guys" that
should have been shared with my mom.

—Tina, New York

• • • • • • • • •

Before we move on, I'd like to add a couple of thoughts on opposite-gender friendships. I have gone back and forth on this issue over the years. After all, our friends are our friends regardless of gender. We wouldn't want to dump a friend just because he or she is of the opposite sex. However, it is easy to fall into a trap in which our opposite-gender friends are meeting needs for us that our significant other could or should be meeting. Don't worry about opposite-gender friends too much when you're dating, but if your relationship is getting serious, watch for the telltale sign of possible trouble. If your significant other is confiding in an opposite-gender friend more than they are in you, that's a major red flag because that behavior isn't just going to "switch off" after you get engaged. That pattern will continue unless something dramatic happens.

The ideal situation is to experience opposite-gender friendships in the context of a relationship with another couple. That's you and your significant other and another couple. Sure, these relationships can be challenging (doubling the number of people involves finding couples who you both really dig, which can be tough), but it is by far a much safer relationship.

So my advice? Watch out for opposite-gender friendships. Danger lurks!

FRIENDS WHO BUILD UP

As important as it is to talk about and come to terms with friends who might drive your significant other crazy, it is just as important to encourage relationships where a friend plays a key role in building up your significant other. Add to that the importance of encouraging your significant other to be the kind of friend who builds up others.

Joanne has both kinds of relationships in her life—some where she is the one who does the building up and others where she is built up by a particular friend. Neither of these kinds of relationships is easy and at times I have been there to encourage Joanne to stick with these friendships. One in particular: Joanne has a dear friend who struggles in her marriage. I won't go into details but things are pretty bad. From time to time Joanne feels like she has nothing to say and can't find words of encouragement for this friend. But Joanne is crucial in this woman's life and it is my role and responsibility to encourage her to stick with it.

Likewise, it may be that you have to hold your significant other's feet to the fire and encourage them to stay involved in a significant relationship that builds them up even though it may be a tough relationship. This can be especially true in mentoring relationships. Sometimes being mentored or being in a relationship where someone speaks truth into your life can be challenging and uncomfortable. In my own life I have had a mentor or two who I wanted to bail on because they were really pushing my buttons on some particular issue. But Joanne has been there to push me to stick with it. She saw the benefit of the relationship even when I didn't. I'm glad I listened to her!

So, this goes hand in hand with the previous section. If you are going to have a role in who your partner's friends are *not*, then you need to be just as active in your support of their healthy friendships.

FRIENDS OF ALL AGES

One of the fun things about being a couple is getting to find couple friends. When we are single most of us have more single friends than couple friends, but as you get serious with your significant other, you might be drawn to find other couples at a similar stage of life.

Joanne and I married in college, so we were surrounded by singles. Sure, there were a lot of dating couples, but there wasn't anyone around who was going through exactly what we were going through. It remained that way until we moved back to Colorado after college.

Once we got there we were determined to meet and fellowship with couples more like us. So we started a young couples Sunday school class at our church. Surprisingly, there were about two dozen other couples who were looking for something just like this. So every Sunday we would meet to talk about "couples stuff." And at least once a week we would gather in small groups to share a meal and study the Bible. This group became a lifeline for Joanne and me during this season. When you are a young couple, married or not, you go through a lot. You are figuring out what it means to be attached to this other person. You're learning how to communicate, you're having fights, and you're figuring out the money stuff—all of it put together can feel pretty overwhelming.

Other couples at your age and stage are going through the same thing. Being with them and talking with them is a form of peer mentoring. As they discover things that help them move together through the sometimes choppy water, they can share that information and hope with you. And you have the opportunity to return the favor by sharing your experience with them. Being in these kinds of relationships is invaluable for a young couple. So seek out people at your age and stage who you can share life with. It'll be well worth it!

But don't limit yourself to couples your age. Early in our relationship Joanne and I met a couple through work who were quite a bit older than we were—somewhere in their mid-forties. This couple had an infectious nature and we were just drawn to them. They were kind enough to make us a part of their lives for a season. These friends had three children, a great home, and a church they loved. They would have us over to their house frequently, which was invaluable time for Joanne and me.

This older couple was able to show us a vision of what the future could be like. We lived in a tiny apartment and couldn't conceive of owning a home someday, but being around them made us realize that having a home might be in our future. They had these beautiful kids, and Joanne and I hadn't even thought about kids, but seeing them interact with theirs and having a chance to connect with them ourselves opened our eyes to what it might be like to have kids of our own. And their marriage served as an example too. All in all they served as role models and gave us something to shoot for years down the road.

I can't tell you how important this relationship was. It painted a picture of our future that we couldn't have imagined on our own and gave us encouragement to strive for those things relationally. I can't recommend enough finding an older couple to be part of your life as a young couple. In some relationships, your parents can fill part of this role—you can learn a lot from them! But it is just as important, if not more so, to find another couple whose relationship you respect and who can model good things for you. If nothing else, it will provide a lot of opportunities for you and your significant other to talk through questions and observations that come from spending time with this older couple.

Don't be afraid to ask an older couple to take on this role in your lives. If you are involved in a church, you are hopefully surrounded by mature, married couples. Simply ask a couple to spend some time with you. In my experience, older couples are happy to oblige. You may be fortunate enough to go to a church with an active small group program, which provides another great opportunity to meet a couple who is further down the road than you are.

Isolation is a killer in a young and developing relationship. If you feel like you don't need couple friends your age or couples who are further down the road than you, that's a red flag. We all need other people to provide examples and to speak into our lives. If either you or your significant other are unwilling or uninterested in doing something like this, you need to take the time to uncover why. Don't drag your feet. This is something both of you need to be excited to pursue.

COMMUNITY

One of the myths that we believe in intense romantic relationships is that our significant other represents everything we need as far as relationships go. We assume that because we love them so much that other friendships and maybe even our communities don't hold as significant a role in our day-to-day experience. But I am here to tell you that, as much as you might feel otherwise, there is no substitute for community.

When I was twenty-seven, I was on a business trip when I started to experience pains in my abdomen. At first I didn't think anything of it, took some Pepto-Bismol, and headed to the airport to fly home. By the time the plane was in the air I was in excruciating pain. The plane landed and I somehow made it to my connecting flight from Denver to Colorado Springs, only to find that the flight had been canceled. So they put all of us on a bus for the sixty-mile trip to the Colorado Springs Airport. Joanne picked me up there and by this point I was screaming in pain. She drove me to the emergency room and I spent the next thirty days in the hospital with a series of problems and complications that involved two major surgeries.

This was certainly an out-of-the-ordinary event. But it illustrated to Joanne and me why community is so important. Our friends from church rallied around us. They visited constantly, checking to see if Joanne needed anything. They brought her food. They prayed tirelessly. And when I finally got out of the hospital and the medical bills started pouring in, they even helped to cover some of the expense.

If everything goes just like you expect it to, you might not see the need or the place of community. But when things go wrong and when you face life's challenges, it is often community that allows you to get through it. So think about this: if you had a crisis in the middle of the night, how many people could you call for help? At times in our relationship Joanne and I would have had to answer, "probably none." That was a scary realization for us.

As a serious couple, it's not too soon to be thinking about and seeking out community. Church is a great place to start. Just like in your serious relationship, you want to be equally yoked with other believers. Church provides that. And be tenacious! I don't know how many young couples Joanne and I have come across who tell us that they just can't find community in their church. We ask a few questions and it becomes clear that they are waiting for community to find them. They hang back waiting for someone to stick out a hand and make them feel welcome.

Joanne and I always tell them, "To find community, you have to be community." What that means is that if you take the first step to get involved, if you meet people and strike up conversations, extend an invitation to a meal, I can almost guarantee you that community is yours.

It's never too soon to start. Even as a dating couple you can begin to meet other couples in your age and stage of life. What's even better is that you may be able to find some older couples who can come alongside as you wrestle through what it means to be a godly couple.

DISCOVERY QUESTIONS

1. Who are your closest friends? Does your significant other know them? Do they get along?

2. How have your relationships with your closest friends changed as a result of a serious relationship? How do you think they feel about that? How do you feel about it?

3. What are your three most significant friendships? How do you think they might be affected if you take your relationship with your significant other to the next step?

4. What need(s) do your closest friends fill that your significant other can't or won't?

5. If you were to count on your significant other to meet a need that is unrealistic for them to fulfill, what result might that produce in your relationship?

6. Do you have a friend who drives your significant other crazy? What is it about this friend that your significant other can't stand? How does that make you feel?

7. What is it about this friend that you love so much? How would you explain it to your significant other?

8. Would you be willing to let your significant other point out a friend who may not be good for you or who is dragging you down?

9. Have you ever had to tell your significant other that you think a friend is not good for them? How did it go? If you had it to do again, how would it be different?

10. What relationship do you see in your significant other's life that you would want to encourage them in? What benefit do you see it providing in their life?

11. How do you think you might seek out relationships with other couples at the same age and stage that you are in? What tangible benefits might you experience?

12. Do you have an older couple in your life? If so, what do they bring to your relationship? If not, can you think of an older couple you would like to start a relationship with? How do you think you might be able to connect with them?

13. Have you been a part of a community that has come to your rescue or provided other support? Have you been a part of a community that provided support for someone else? What were those experiences like?

14. On a scale of one to ten, how much do you value community? How much does your significant other value

community? How do you interpret the similarity or difference in your answers?

RED FLAGS

- If you or your significant other don't see the value of community, if you aren't willing to seek out others who can come alongside you, and if you feel like all you need is each other, that's a red flag.
- If your friends can't be friends with each other or if you can't stand his friends and he can't stand yours, then that's a red flag. Just as you bring your family into any serious relationship, you also bring your friends.
- If you can't even talk about why a particular friend might not be a good or healthy friend, then that's a red flag. If you are serious about your relationship, then everything is on the table.
- If all your friends are your age and you don't have any older and wiser friends, and worse, if you don't have any interest in making these kinds of friends, then that's a red flag. God brings people into our lives to help us navigate through tough times and it is to our extreme benefit to allow him to make that happen.
- If you aren't willing to stick out your hand, meet people, and begin friendships, then you can't expect to find community. If you are unwilling to make the first move and if you are content to sit back and wait for community to find you, then that's a red flag.

CHAPTER 6

What the Heck Is a Yoke?

FAITH AND RELIGION

First, he must be a Christian. It's hard enough
trying to make a relationship work these days, let
alone if you put another obstacle in your way.

—EMILY, ARIZONA

f we were putting these chapters in order of importance, this one would be first. The Bible is pretty clear: we aren't to be "unequally yoked" (see 2 Cor. 6:14). In other words, we are both to be believers. Simple as that. But it isn't always that simple, is it? After all, the heart wants what the heart wants. Sometimes we are attracted to and get into romantic relationships with people who we know aren't believers. I can tell you that this will only lead to heartache.

It is easy when we are attracted to someone who isn't a believer to think about "dating them into the kingdom," that somehow we will be able to share our faith over time and they will come to believe what we believe. I won't lie to you, I have seen it happen. But I can also tell you stories of other couples who after years of relationship and even marriage are still miles apart on faith issues. And in almost all those cases, it is a serious issue in their lives.

UNEQUALLY YOKED

So maybe you're thinking that you are only dating—it's not like you've decided to get married—so the fact that your significant other isn't a believer is no big deal. Well, it is a big deal. Even with dating, there are still sets of moral guidelines that come with being a Christian that it will be hard to keep if you don't both support them. And if you are of marrying age, why would you bother to date someone and invest time in a relationship that isn't going anywhere? What's the point?

Think about the potential heartache for you and your significant other if you know deep down that this relationship doesn't have what it takes to go the distance. What if he or she falls in love with you and eventually you have to make the decision whether to marry someone who doesn't share your faith in Christ or to dump him or her? Neither of those are good options. So why would you put yourself in a position to have to make one of those two decisions?

I have also seen a number of couples where the believer in the couple ignores the reality of the situation and ascribes a "spirituality" to their partner that simply doesn't exist. If you can't be entirely honest about your own faith and if your significant other can't do the same, that's a massive red flag.

A few actions or conversations will indicate to you, even early on, whether the person you are attracted to is a believer. Do they go to church? Are they involved in a small group or Bible study? Do they ever share spiritual thoughts or truths? Is there evidence of prayer? I know this all sounds almost like snooping, but it is of such great importance that you have to make sure.

I have a friend who fell in love with a guy who wasn't a believer. In fact, not only was he not a believer, but he was an atheist. How crazy is that? But she was in love with him and when he asked her to marry him, she said yes. Now the hope would be that as she lived out her faith in their marriage that he might warm to the idea of Christianity and that, over time, he might even come to a saving faith. Guess what? It hasn't happened. And in many ways his faithlessness has been more of a challenge to her faith then her faith has been to his godlessness.

She goes to church sometimes but doesn't have a real church home. After all, it is hard to go to church by yourself on a Sunday morning when your spouse doesn't want to join you. She has participated in Bible studies and those have been rich experiences for her, but again she does that without any support.

The reality of this situation is that this sister in Christ has a faith that is developing at a fractional rate of what it could be doing if she were equally yoked and supported in her faith. A spiritually nurturing environment helps us to grow and flourish in our faith. One that is barren makes it very difficult to grow to our spiritual potential.

It's hard to watch. Her motive is good and her desire to grow is there but she is oppressed to some extent by her context. I really wouldn't wish that on any believer. It hasn't only affected issues of faith and development as a believer, but has leached into every other issue in their lives. I honestly don't know how they make a go of it other than the fact that as a committed believer, she doesn't believe in divorce.

Get the picture? Don't for a second convince yourself that faith isn't the central issue in any marriage. You can tell yourself that you are in agreement on so many other issues—money, kids, communication, friendships—but at the end of the day, if you aren't on the same page when it comes to Christ, ultimately you will struggle more than you ever would if one of those other issues wasn't in accord.

How are you going to spend your money? As a believer you are going to want to give some of it to the church. Is your non-Christian partner going to be cool with that? If not, how will you solve it? Will you give in or fight for it? How about kids? Are they going to be raised to believe what you believe or what your spouse believes? And even if they are cool with you raising the kids to believe what you believe, how are you going to explain to them the fact that their other parent doesn't believe what the rest of the family believes? And what about commitment to marriage? As a believer you are committed to seeing it through thick and thin, and worse. But nothing binds the nonbeliever in the same way. It is more an issue of personal choice and less one of moral, spiritual conviction.

Finally, think about this. C. S. Lewis has said that we need to view every person as an eternal being: one that will either spend eternity in heaven with God or eternity in hell. How could you live with yourself if the person you loved most in the world was part of the latter group? I can tell you that it would tear me up every day.

EVEN WHEN YOU BOTH BELIEVE

I recently heard about a woman who was a strong believer who fell in love with a man who said he was also a Christian. As she spent time with him and as they grew closer, she noticed that there didn't seem to be much in the way of behavior or fruit that came forth from this guy's faith. In fact, based on what she saw, she really wouldn't have been able to place this guy as a believer. He went to church with her when she asked and they said a prayer over meals, but that was about it. But he said he was a Christian and because she loved him so much she took him at his word.

Fast-forward about five years. This couple is married but things aren't going well. She has continued her Christian walk and has sought a deeper, more meaningful relationship with Christ; he has gone in quite the other direction. It's not that he has out-and-out rejected God, but he shows little or no interest in spirituality. And this is causing problems. The friend who told me this story explained that it's like they're on two roads headed in sort of the same direction but moving ever more steadily apart. Not a good situation. And it is breeding resentment on both sides.

So, what's the point here? When we fall in love, it is easy to turn off some of our senses. We can turn off our eyes to the mannerisms we see in our significant other that may make us uncomfortable. We can turn off our ears to the thoughts and concerns of friends and family. We can turn off our speech, afraid to say something that might offend or drive a wedge between us and the person we care so much about. But that's the last thing we should be doing when we start to get serious with someone.

· · · · · · · · ·

One thing I did pay attention to was
the devotional life of my intended. It was strong
and consistent, not just for show. We all have
our ebbs and flows, but if a person has
developed the discipline and longing to be with
the Lord, it will remain . . . always.

—TAMARA, OREGON

· · · · · · · · ·

It has been said that love is blind (and deaf and dumb too). However, that is tragic, especially when it comes to the spiritual standing of a potential spouse. I can't say this with enough passion or seriousness: turn on all your senses when it comes to discerning the faith commitment and spiritual maturity and growth of someone you are falling in love with. This area may be the single most important determinant of relational success, so to ignore it is the worst of ideas and the biggest of red flags.

So what does it mean to engage your senses and your discernment when it comes to the spiritual life of your significant other? Well, it doesn't mean sitting them down in a chair and grilling them for three or four hours under hot lights. It means starting a dialogue, an ongoing conversation that will reveal their heart and yours. You owe that to a partner just as they owe it to you, and you can't ask them to do something you're not willing to undertake. Obviously a helpful skill in all this is the ability to ask questions based on curiosity and observation.

Start simple. Most of us who have been believers for any amount of time are pretty comfortable sharing our testimonies and this is a great place to start. I know, it sounds pretty formal and unromantic to recite your coming-to-faith story, but it is foundational. When you hear their story, really listen for the heart of your significant other. Ask thoughtful questions and draw them out.

Then observe and ask questions. If you make spiritual discussion a normal part of your relationship, then it will be easy to get clarification when things don't seem to mesh. If it's not an ongoing discussion, it can make the other person feel like you're grilling them. An example: your significant other loves Jesus, no question about that. But when they get behind the wheel it's like a whole other person emerges—an angry, aggressive person. If you are used to talking about spiritual things, it'd be easy to ask, "So how does this behavior fit with what you believe and how you want to live?" Fair question. If you aren't used to having this sort of conversation, then your query could feel heavy-handed and accusatory. So get in the habit of discussing your spiritual life.

Finally, affirm positive sightings of the person's faith life and their desire to grow. This kind of affirmation balances out some of the hard questions you might need to ask along the way. If you are able to say, "Here's something I really admire about your Christian walk," that will go a long way toward building a rapport that will support the other heavy lifting you may need to do as you seek to be not just a companion, but a spiritual partner.

CHURCH

Joanne and I both grew up in church. Every Sunday, rain or shine, we were there. I think my parents were a little less insistent on my church attendance than Joanne's parents were, but regardless, through high school we were in church on Sundays. But truthfully it wasn't something we felt like we had a lot of choice in, and as is the case for most kids who feel forced into something, when they get the chance to rebel, they are going to. And rebel we did.

When we went to college together, we went to church very little. Sure, from time to time we would go to a small community church near our college in Spokane, Washington, but that was maybe once a month. We just didn't go. Not that it was anything we were very intentional about. I wish now, looking back, that we had talked about why we weren't getting involved in a church community instead of just letting it slide.

As a dating couple over those years, our lack of participation in church cut us off from all sorts of growth and support opportunities. We definitely could have benefited from Christian relationships with peers and older couples who could have encouraged us and spoken truth into our lives. Plus, we always benefit from worshiping regularly and hearing God's Word preached from the pulpit.

Maybe you and your significant other go to church together. If so, I applaud you! You are making a great decision and starting a habit that will serve you well throughout your relationship. Undoubtedly you are surrounded with people who care for you, who want the best for you, and who can provide you counsel and accountability.

• • • • • • • • •

I wish we had put God first in our lives
rather than "living" the way we wanted to.
—SAMANTHA, ILLINOIS

• • • • • • • • •

It's even fine at this point if you and your significant other are at different churches. Still a good thing.

Now for the not-so-hot option: what if one or both of you don't go to church? This has all kinds of implications for your relationship as you go forward. It's easy to *say* that you are going to do things or value things in the future that you don't do or value today. "If we get engaged, we'll commit to a church." Or, "If we end up getting married, church will become a priority for us." Don't count on it. Getting engaged or getting married doesn't make you a different person. The patterns and habits you have as a single person or as someone in a dating relationship aren't likely to just automatically change.

If you both aren't going to church, and if the relationship is getting serious, think about going to church together. If you aren't up for that yet, at least make sure that you both are attending your home churches. If one or both of you aren't in a body of believers, that's a red flag.

So let's assume that you are going to make the good decision to go to church. Wow, there are a lot out there to choose from—something like three hundred thousand in the United States. And they are as diverse as you can imagine. So finding one where you both are comfortable—that you can participate in and that provides you the best opportunity for growth and community—might not be that easy. But there are a few steps that might make it easier.

First, get feedback from friends or family. When our family moved back to Colorado, we didn't want to spend Sundays picking churches out of the phone book, so we called friends to find out what churches they recommended. After visiting only four churches, we found the church that we are still members of today. That's pretty good considering the thousands of churches we had to choose from in Denver.

Second, think about what denomination you have experience or comfort with. This can be a tough one if you and your significant other come from different denominations. Getting a book on denominations isn't a bad idea; it will allow you to do a little research before trying a church. I have flipped through the *Handbook of Denominations in the United States* by Frank Mead, Samuel Hill, and Craig Atwood many times. (It's actually really interesting reading.) Maybe you will be one of those lucky couples who grew up in the same denomination and can easily find a church home in the denomination. Perhaps you didn't grow up in a church, in which case you are probably going to have to visit a larger number of churches before you figure out what's different about them and which one is a better fit for you as a couple.

When you start visiting churches together, be prepared to pay attention and to talk about what you liked and disliked about the church. You will probably have to visit more than once to really get a sense of a church.

Keep in mind that finding a church together is an exercise in building your relationship. Keep those channels of communication open, be prepared to ask a lot of questions, do your research, but most of all, commit together that you are going to be in church on Sundays. I've never known a new couple who didn't benefit from it. I know of plenty of couples who were adversely affected by not doing it.

Back to the story of Joanne and me in college. It took a while after graduation for us to get back in the swing of going to church. We bounced around a little but finally ended up at a church we both really liked. Even with that being the case, it took us a while to be like-minded on the importance of church—Joanne has always had a higher commitment to participating in church. But now we are on the same page—and it only took fifteen years! I totally wish we would have gotten on the same page back when we were just getting started. It would have been of great benefit to our relationship and to our growth.

THE DISCIPLINES

I never would have viewed the spiritual disciplines—prayer, quiet time, Scripture reading and memorization, etc.—as important before Joanne and I got together, and to be honest this is one of the areas that we are probably mostly apart on in our marriage. Still struggling with coming together on these disciplines after years of marriage makes me realize how much we would have benefited from thinking and talking through this topic before we got engaged or married. Now I can tell you that this isn't a deal breaker—after all, many of us have unique and special ways of living out our relationship with God—but I can say that being able to hold some disciplines in common certainly would strengthen a relationship.

Joanne's folks are a positive example of how this can work. For years and years, they have been reading the Bible together and praying together almost every day. They have spiritual unity around this common practice. Just by being around them, I can tell that it does a lot to keep them on the same page, not only relationally but spiritually as well. It helps them transcend the day-to-day and focus on the eternal. I can't tell you the countless people who they have faithfully prayed for over the years.

I am embarrassed to say that Joanne and I don't do much of that. Yes, we go to church together and we pray with our kids together. We pray for each other but rarely with each other. I wish we prayed together more often, but for some reason we just haven't made it happen.

I want something better for you! I want you and your significant other to start off on the right foot and begin to talk about and practice the spiritual disciplines that mean the most to you.

DISCOVERY QUESTIONS

1. Is your significant other a Christian? How much focus do the two of you put on your faith in the context of your relationship?

2. If you are in a relationship with a non-Christian, why is that? What do you think is the potential for the future of your relationship?

3. Do you have a friend who is "unequally yoked"? What are the challenges that they face in this relationship? How would you counsel them if they asked you about it?

4. Do you think you have turned off any of your senses when it comes to addressing spiritual issues in your relationship? Which ones and for what reason?

5. Have you shared your testimony with your significant other? Have they shared theirs with you? If not, what might it take for this to happen?

6. If you were to affirm one spiritual trait of your significant other (assuming they are a believer), what would it be?

7. Do you and your significant other regularly attend church? Do you go to church together? One way or another, how has that affected your relationship?

8. What view on church do you currently hold that you think might change once your relationship goes to the next level? Why do you think it will change?

9. If you have visited one another's churches, what were your impressions? What did you like and dislike? What sort of church might you like to attend together if things get serious?

10. What spiritual disciplines are important to you? What about for your significant other? What do they bring to your faith life?

⚑ RED FLAGS

- If your significant other isn't a believer, this is the red flag of all red flags. Period.

- If there is no evidence of spirituality or growth or fruit in the life of your significant other, even though they profess Christ, then you need to do a little digging. If they aren't open to sharing their heart about what they believe and why, that's a red flag.

- If you both aren't committed to a church that you regularly attend, that's a red flag. Additionally, if you really hate each other's churches and can't conceive of the kind of church you might enjoy going to together, that's a red flag.

- If you can't talk about your faith journey and the practices that are important to you: red flag.

•

CHAPTER 7

Is "Barista" a Profession?

CAREER AND CALLING

*I wish I would have known what it would
really be like to be married to a farmer.
The financial considerations that go
into being a farm family, whew!*

—MARY, KANSAS

Why do careers matter? He'll have his job, she'll have hers, and away we go. But these days, one or the other in a relationship may decide on a career or respond to a calling that has a dramatic impact on them as a couple.

Joanne and I know a young couple not yet married who are working through this issue. Both go to a Christian college and feel called to a life in ministry. He feels called to the local church and would like to follow in his dad's footsteps and become a pastor. She feels called to the mission field and would love to be a missionary in Central America. Now both of these callings are awesome! The local church? The mission field? Great stuff! But for this couple it is pulling them in two different directions, and they are really wrestling with what it means that even though they are in love, God seems to be calling them to two different paths. This couple is well on their way to working through this. Their relationship is by no means doomed, and by the time you read this, it is likely that they will be married. The key for them has been flexibility and working toward a win-win. But that doesn't mean this has been easy.

We know another couple who is seriously dating and about to face a similar challenge. He is a teacher and she is studying to be a dental hygienist, which is not really what she wants to do. When you put her on the spot she'll tell you that what she wants to do is be a stay-at-home mom. This couple currently lives in one of the most expensive places in the country, and the chances that they are going to be able to fulfill both their ideals is slim—him teaching and her staying at home with a number of kids. So what should they do about that? Obviously they both have dreams and it would be tough for either one of them to just give those up—for her to give up hopes of being a stay-at-home mom or for him to abandon teaching to get a high paying, high-stress job. So what should they do?

It's not too early to talk about career and calling when you are dating. The conversation can give you a good sense as to how well someone has thought out this important aspect of their life and will let you know if their hopes and dreams are compatible with yours. At an early stage of a dating relationship, this talk is mostly informational. You are interested in sharing your vision of what you may feel called to do or what job you think you would like to have, and your significant other can do the same. It's not likely to change anything for you as you exchange this information. After all, at this early stage it would be foolish to start to think about giving up your dream or your calling to make way for your significant other. If this progresses, there will be plenty of time to think about that.

More than informational, a person's choice of career or their sense of calling will reveal a lot about who they are. If they are at an age or stage where they don't have to choose a career path, how they think about the upcoming decision is a great revealer of what is going on behind the scenes in this person's life. Are they anxious about the decision? Are they making tentative plans? Are they open to the leading of the Spirit? Take the time to talk about where you both think you're headed in your career. Ask clarifying questions about not only the "what" but the "why." Really listen. If you do, you will learn a lot about the person. Is their primary career goal to make money? Help people? Follow a passion?

Again, if your ideas about work and the future don't line up, that doesn't have to be a deal breaker. Many couples as they come together are willing to make changes and sacrifices for the sake of the relationship. But for some, the love that drives this decision starts to wear thin as they find themselves looking for, accepting, and working in a job that they hate.

CALLING OR CAREER?

Anyone can get a *job*. In fact, tons of people get by simply doing a job. Some people have a *career*, which is a job with future plans and expectations. A career implies a path. Start here, take this next step, and end up somewhere. A calling is even bigger and more involved than that. *Calling* often implies a sense of destiny or a desire that God has put on your heart.

Jobs are easy because you can do this or do that and in the long run switching jobs isn't all that big a deal. I have a friend who works at a coffee shop in Seattle. She and her new husband decided to make a move from the south side of the city to the north. So she quit her coffee shop job down there and got a new one when she got to their new location. No big deal.

Changing careers would be five times more difficult. The same friend in Seattle happens to be a great actress. She works at the coffee shop to make ends meet, but her career is acting in local theater, directing plays, and working in media. She is really, really good at it. Now, if this couple had decided to move to a tiny little town for one reason or another, that would necessitate a career change on her part. Getting that coffee shop job? No big deal. Moving to a community without a thriving arts program? Big deal. Make sense?

Changing one's calling, however, is almost impossible. I have seen it happen, but once God puts an idea in your mind and a desire on your heart, it would be hard to change that, because really, only God can change it. Same friend in Seattle: her calling is to use theater for education. She loves to perform with a purpose. She has started a theater group that travels to schools to do performances that help teach science. This is where she gets the most satisfaction. Clearly it takes a little more than just doing this to make ends meet, but it is doing this that fulfills her calling. Asking her to stop doing it would be for her to lose a little of her soul.

MAKING ENDS MEET

Now for the nitty-gritty. Career and calling have a major effect on lifestyle, and this has to be taken into account when you are thinking and talking about how a life together might look. Think back to our couple with the woman who desires to be a stay-at-home mom and her boyfriend who wants to be a teacher. For this couple, living where they do, they could not make ends meet with this arrangement. So they have a few choices to make, none of which are necessarily bad. The first is that they can change their ideas about career. He could get a different, higher paying job. She could decide that working part-time as a dental hygienist could still fit with the kind of mom she wants to be.

The second is that they could delay their plans for a few years until the conditions are right. Maybe they hold off on kids while they build up a nest egg that would allow her to have the future she sees for herself. This is something that they could definitely talk about and might represent a best-case scenario for them.

The other option is that they could move somewhere less expensive. This option again merits discussion. Of course they love where they live and they have friends and community there, so they have to weigh their desires against their realities and move forward.

You would be amazed at the number of people who get married without really knowing how they are going to make it. Joanne and I were among them. As I mentioned, we were very young when we got married. Our parents made it clear that if and when we decided to get married, we were on our own financially. We were making an adult decision and supporting ourselves was part of entering into that adult relationship.

• • • • • • • • •

I want to know what things are going to be like down the road: where he'll work, where I'll work, what happens when we have kids. We know what we're doing now, but what is he going to be like five years from now, and how is he going to handle job changes, family changes, and the things that life throws at us?

—Hannah, Texas

• • • • • • • •

But we were in college. We didn't have jobs that made much money—Joanne worked part-time as a graphic designer and I worked in the college bookstore. I guess we thought we would just figure it out. Making ends meet was not as important as being together. The result: a lot of worry. We spent a bunch of time stressing out about the fact that we didn't have enough money. The other outcome: we spent almost entirely on credit and amassed a debt that took eight years to pay off. This debt fueled more worry. I can remember getting up in the middle of the night, unable to sleep because of financial pressure, and calling the credit card company to check our balance, trying to figure out if we would be able to make our next payment.

I tell you all this because I don't want to underplay the importance of figuring out how you will support yourselves if you end up together. You may already be supporting yourself now, but be aware that extra expenses come with married life and you have to anticipate and prepare for them. Again this need not be a deal breaker in an emerging relationship. What it does mean is that you have something to talk about.

WHERE TO LIVE

In this age of Internet dating, it is easier than ever before to maintain long-distance relationships, so it is possible that your significant other lives far away. As you get closer together relationally, you will need to have a discussion about where you will live.

I have friends who lived on opposite sides of a major metropolitan area. She lived and worked in the north and he lived and worked in the south. They got married and because she owned a home, they decided he would move north. Problem is, his job is still in the south, which is now over an hour drive each way, every day. It's not just that it's a drag to make the drive, but it also has a significant financial impact. He has paid as much as six hundred dollars a month for gas to commute.

So when you get to the point of talking about where you'll live, you need to make a list. On that list put all the things that are important to you about your location, down to the smallest detail. Do you want to be close to your job? Write it down. Do you want to be near your church? Write it down. Close to restaurants, shopping, the library, or whatever? Write it down. Then start the conversation about where you might live, trying to meet all those requirements.

It may seem easiest for one member of the relationship to just move in with the other after they are married, but count the cost. You're in this relationship for the long haul, and while it may be inconvenient to move, it's better to be in a suitable location for the both of you. I used to commute an hour each way to work when we lived in San Diego. We did that on purpose (believe it or not) so that our family could live near the beach and close to my favorite aunt and uncle. For a while it made sense, but honestly, after a couple of years making this drive, it got old. I was losing family time with so many hours on the road. Something had to change.

We weren't in a position to move, so I had to make significant changes in my job to bring my life into balance. Fortunately I worked for a company that was OK with me working at home a few days a week (that helped a lot!). But in hindsight, we didn't really count the costs of where we wanted to live versus what was best for our family. Since then, we have moved twice and each time we have had exhaustive lists of what location would be our perfect fit. Both moves have been great as a result.

So take the time to have this conversation. It can actually be pretty fun because it will allow you to dream together a little. You'll be able to talk about what might be just the right fit.

DISCOVERY QUESTIONS

1. What do you feel called to? Have you thought much about how your careers might draw you closer together or maybe move you further apart?

2. If someone put you on the spot, could you articulate your significant other's career path, their desire for what they will spend the next season of life doing or pursuing? What would it take for you to be able to answer this question?

3. What would you be willing to do, give up, or delay to make ends meet if your relationship leads to marriage?

4. What additional expenses do you think you'll have if you end up together? Are you prepared to handle that?

5. Have you talked about how to make ends meet? What challenges might you face?

6. What are your priorities when deciding where to live? Do you want to be close to family? Near your job? Close to church? What are your significant other's priorities?

▶ RED FLAGS

- If you or your significant other have no real thoughts about what you want to do with your life, if either of you just scrape by in a job you hate, this is going to have a big impact on your future. If you or they don't have a plan or a goal, that's a red flag.

- If your career plans are pulling the two of you in opposite directions, don't expect that taking your relationship to the next level will automatically resolve those issues. It will likely make them more challenging. If you can't talk about your career plans and goals, or if you're not willing or able to bend, that's a red flag.

- If you have callings that seem incompatible, you are going to have a very difficult time figuring out how to address that. Calling runs deep and is often given to us by God. It would be unfair or unreasonable to expect that one of you is just going to roll over on this thing that God put in your heart. If you are headed in different directions as a result of calling, that's a red flag.

- If you have no way of making ends meet or if you don't have a plan about how to make that happen, then that's red flag territory.

•

CHAPTER 8

Minivan or Mini Cooper?

CHILDREN AND FAMILY LIFE

*I thought he would be more open to talking about
kids and starting a family, but it was a topic
that he didn't want to talk about at first. It took
some time for us to get on the same page and
there were some hurt feelings along the way.*

—JENNA, COLORADO

When it came to the "kids" discussion, Joanne and I were pretty much on the same page in the beginning—we were too young to think about kids when we were engaged just out of high school and married in college. We were both aware that the discussion was a ways off.

Some discussions are better left until after you're engaged or even married. And some discussions might not be appropriate, or even possible, until you are a few years into marriage. So when we talk about kids, understand that whatever you discuss early in your relationship isn't the final word. Circumstances change when you get engaged and they change further once you are married. The discussion of how many children to have is even likely to continue through several years of marriage, up until a couple decides that they're done having kids! But this is a big topic and it's a good idea to get a sense of what your significant other is thinking. I have seen a number of couples for whom this has become a major issue in their marriage. It might not have kept them from getting married, but it certainly has made it a little more difficult to stay married.

A QUESTION TO REVISIT

I know a couple who very early in their relationship decided that if they ended up together they would never, ever have kids. This was mostly driven by the guy—he's just not into children. His girlfriend and future wife went along with him on this issue, agreeing that they never needed to have a child. But then something changed. As she got older and as her friends started having children, she started to want a baby of her own. He was adamant, however, that kids were not an option. This began to drive a wedge into their relationship, and it continues to be an issue of contention.

This scenario contains all sorts of problems, but let's look at two that could have been addressed beforehand. First, she was never convinced that not having kids was the way to go. She was in love and wanted to get married and said what he wanted to hear so that they could be together. How she regrets that now!

Being honest at every stage of your relationship is so critical. Saying what you think your significant other wants to hear is only going to cause trouble later.

· · · · · · · · · ·

We both wanted to have kids, but I grew up
in a large family and I thought we'd have at least
three kids, but her pregnancy was so tough
that we ended up having only one.
That was a major adjustment from how I thought
things were going to be. I guess you have to
be prepared that what you want and
what God wants may be different.

—ALEX, UTAH

· · · · · · · · · ·

Second, as a dating couple, they made a decision that they weren't willing to revisit. In everything we've talked about to this point in the book, you have to realize that open discussion is necessary not only initially, but also at every step along the way. You aren't really making firm decisions as a dating couple as much as you are starting to get a sense of how the other person is wired. It wouldn't make sense for a dating couple to say, "We're not going to have kids," and never expect to revisit the decision. People change. That's part of the beauty of being in a relationship. You are attracted to a person who is going to grow and develop and mature and continue to be interesting, engaging, and attractive. Yes, you may love the person you are with right now. That's great.

But change and growth are necessary—they prevent people and relationships from becoming stale.

You have to realize that ideas you have today may change. Subjects you feel strongly about may become less important; conversely, issues you don't care about at all today may become very important. That needs to be understood from the get-go. To say, "We'll never have kids" is crazy, even if one of you already knows that they can't parent children naturally. You can say that, at this particular point in time, that's not what you're interested in, but you are going to change, and you need to be open to your options. It's important that you keep this issue and others open for discussion. You don't want to create a bunch of "off-limits" areas in your relationship. I haven't found a single issue in my own marriage that can be discussed and put to bed for good. Almost every issue needs to be revisited from time to time in order to make sure that Joanne and I are still on the same page.

KIDS AND LIFESTYLE

This principle of keeping discussions open is important, but let's get back to the discussion itself. Just like the callings and careers discussion, it is important to realize that this particular topic of having kids has a lot to do with lifestyle. If you haven't noticed by now, almost all of these important discussions are interrelated and affect one another.

For example, maybe your significant other grew up in a large family and has a vision for the future in which you have a large family with kids running around everywhere. That implies that someone is going to have to stay home with those kids (who can afford daycare for that many little ones!). So the issue isn't simply to have a big family or not to have a big family, it is about how you will live your life.

For Joanne and me the discussion became more about the life we wanted to lead early in our relationship and where kids fit into that. We knew a couple of things: we wanted to own a home, we wanted to be out of debt, and we wanted the option of having Joanne stay home with the baby if that became something she was interested in doing. That was our discussion, instead of the should we/shouldn't we have kids discussion. For Joanne and me that meant that we were married for about seven years before Audrey came into the picture. And the timing was just right. We had accomplished all those things that we had agreed to as a couple.

Have the lifestyle discussion when it comes to kids, just the way you would have a careers and callings discussion. Do you want to pursue a particular career? Do you want to travel and see some of the world? Do you want to continue your education or get an advanced degree? All this has bearing on the kids discussion, and even if you aren't talking specifically about kids, you can easily read between the lines and get a sense of this. And remember, a lot of this discussion will be shaped by being able to talk about your family of origin and what your family looked like growing up.

KIDS AND YOUR SIGNIFICANT OTHER

One last thing: it can be fun and informative to see how your significant other acts around kids. Having your own children and loving and caring for them is very different than spending time with someone else's kids, but nevertheless, the situation can be pretty eye opening.

My wife volunteered in children's ministry from an early age. First she helped out in the nursery at church, and then she taught Sunday school when she was older. It was clear to me early on that she loved kids and would probably make a pretty decent parent.

And she got to see a glimpse of that with me. When we were in college, we had friends who would ask us to babysit their infant from time to time. As I held and rocked the baby, I could see Joanne light up a little because I think she envisioned what I might look like holding one of our own kids someday. I even changed diapers, which I'm sure thrilled her.

This is all part of our observations about our potential spouse. We keep our eyes and ears open, we pick up on subtle cues, and from that we can get a pretty good idea of what our future might look like. Kids are a big part of this!

DISCOVERY QUESTIONS

1. Do you see kids in your future? Does your significant other?

2. Even if you have a clear sense of whether or not you want kids in the future, is it a question that you are willing to revisit? How about your significant other?

3. How does the family situation that you grew up in affect your own thoughts about kids? How about for your significant other?

4. Do you relate well to kids? Does your significant other?
5. What lifestyle choices will have the biggest influence on your choice to parent and when? Do you and your significant other agree about those priorities?

▶ RED FLAG

There's really only one red flag in this area: are you and your significant other willing to talk about kids and then revisit the issue again and again as you move through different stages of your relationship? If you or your significant other feels locked into a decision even at this early stage of your relationship, that's a red flag.

•

Are You Seeing What I'm Seeing?

Joanne and I have sat with many dating and engaged couples and talked to them about their relationship and what is coming next for them. Our favorite line in these talks is when a couple says something like, "You know, we've never had a real disagreement." My first thought is always, "Well, maybe it's because you haven't talked about anything serious yet." The reality is that some of the topics in this book will be close to your heart, and chances are some disagreements are going to arise. Don't let that freak you out! Instead, use these topics, questions, and discussions not only to gather information, but also to reveal insights about how you communicate as a couple, especially about stuff you really care about.

OBSERVE YOUR SIGNIFICANT OTHER

Actions speak louder than words (like you've never heard that before). So when you get into this serious relationship, and when you have these serious talks, make sure you turn on your powers of observation. Along with what your significant other says, you have to observe how they live.

For example, when Joanne and I were dating we didn't have a lot of major conversations about many of these topics. We were young and in love and that's all that mattered to us. However, we did have the opportunity to spend a lot of time in each other's homes and around each other's parents, and we learned a lot about each other that way. For example, I came to understand that to Joanne's family, religion was extremely important. They prayed together, did Bible study after meals, and never missed church. From that I could gather that this was going to be important to Joanne because it was ingrained in her. Now we never had a talk about this, but through observation I was able to figure it out. And it turned out to be true—faith and religion are very important to Joanne.

Hanging out with my family, Joanne was able to pick up a few things. For example, my dad was a lavish gift giver. He got a lot of joy out of being able to provide for my mom and me. I got a great bicycle when I was a kid. When I turned sixteen, I got a car for Christmas. When I went to college and expressed an interest in photography, my dad outfitted me completely. Joanne observed all this and was able to make the assumption that I would be generous and enjoy giving gifts as well. And that has proved true. To this day I love to give gifts.

We learned so much being in each other's households, even though we probably couldn't have articulated specifics at the time. This time of observation was critical, especially because we didn't even know that we needed to be talking about these topics.

Even if you don't have the opportunity to spend a lot of time in your significant other's family home, be observant when you are in social settings, when you are around each other's families, and when your significant other talks about work or church. Take it all in and you'll get a pretty good picture of who you are involved with. These observations make the perfect jumping off point for questions. As you observe patterns or idiosyncrasies, follow up at the appropriate time with a question or two. You can say, "I noticed the other day when we were with your parents that they seem to (fill in the blank). What do you think about that? How has that affected you?"

Obviously you need to be tactful when you ask these questions so as not to put your significant other on the spot or make them feel defensive. Unfortunately defensiveness is a somewhat natural reaction, even among people who are relatively open, and especially when you're talking about friends and family. These are relationships that are closely held and no one likes to be challenged on their important relationships. But if these topics become off-limits, if you aren't allowed to follow up on things that you see and experience, then that's a big red flag. After all, you want to be with someone who is open and honest and who has the ability to be introspective and thoughtful.

ASK FOR FEEDBACK

Listening to friends and family about your relationship with your significant other can be complicated. Few people in your life will know your significant other as well as you do, but that doesn't mean that others' opinions and observations aren't valid and shouldn't be taken into account. Your dad may think that no one is good enough for you, or you may have a friend who is jealous and isn't going to give you the straight scoop on his or her observations, but you also have people whom you can trust. They can't make decisions for you, but you can accept their feedback as part of the larger picture.

Joanne and I have a good friend who got married shortly after Joanne and I did. We were really close to this woman and spent quite a bit of time with her and her boyfriend. We were all living on a college campus, so she was surrounded by people who were observing this relationship.

A lot of us had some concerns as the relationship developed. No major concerns—mostly just a feeling that something wasn't quite right, that maybe they were rushing things. But no one said anything. And she didn't solicit anyone's opinion.

They got married and it lasted less than two years. He made some bad choices and they divorced. If that wasn't painful enough, this woman had people telling her, "From the beginning, we really had doubts that this would work but didn't know how to tell you." What a terrible thing to hear! People around her saw things that concerned them, but didn't say anything. Perhaps the heartache and massive fallout from this broken relationship could have been avoided if she had sought feedback from friends and family. Those of us who cared about her blew it too, because solicited or unsolicited, we should have voiced our concerns.

Asking for feedback is tricky because you are likely in love (or close to it) with your significant other, and your tendency is going to be to defend him or her when people have observations that may be less than flattering. We have all seen negatively affected friendships and damaged parent-child relationships when a friend or parent has concerns about our most significant relationship. But you owe it to yourself to take this feedback, to really consider it, to follow up on it, and to potentially make it a source of discussion between you and your significant other.

Tact is key. You don't want to approach your significant other with, "Hey, my mom and dad think you're a jerk!" Nothing good could come from that. So tread lightly, but don't blow off the people who know and love you the most. Failure to want to talk about the feedback is a red flag.

What if you get feedback that you don't like? That's a tough one. You may be in love, you may be planning a future and headed toward getting engaged, and then WHAMMO! A close friend, family member, or parent raises a concern that maybe you haven't seen or haven't been willing to see. Now it's time for some soul searching.

A lot of thought and prayerful consideration have to come into play. As hard as it might be, you have to put yourself in a position of openness to hear and consider the tough stuff that's being said. It may not be entirely correct, but it may not be totally off base either.

If the friend or family member that rains on your parade has been a good source of wisdom and advice for you, you can't just blow them off now. You have to consider the source, and if they have been right a bunch of times, there's reason to believe that they may be right again.

Of course the opposite is true as well. You may have a friend or family member that has an opinion about everything and they are just talking to hear themselves speak. So use discernment about what you're hearing. If the person is trustworthy and reliable and if he or she is truly concerned, there is probably something to what the person's saying. In fact, this person's words might be your deal breaker. If the person giving you advice isn't trustworthy, it's still not a bad idea to listen and consider his or her opinion, but you can't give it the same weight as the words of someone you respect.

BE HONEST WITH YOURSELF

When you fall in love, all sorts of things happen to an otherwise rational person. Some even suggest that your brain chemistry changes when you're in love and that it actually affects your ability to make good judgment calls. Regardless of chemical reactions, it is important to force yourself to think, really think, about the relationship that you're in. It is so easy to get swept up in the feelings and the emotions of a new relationship (or even one that's not so new) and to have those feelings lead to a level of commitment and intimacy that, if you were rational about it, wouldn't make any sense.

Most of us know couples where one or the other of the people in the relationship gets treated terribly, but for whatever reason they stick with it, and defend it when a friend or family member raises concerns. This is heartbreaking to watch. Subjecting oneself to bad treatment is driven by a desire to be loved, to feel special, and to have someone significant in your life, along with a number of other reasons. The reality is that most people in bad relationships have some sense, somewhere way down deep, that they shouldn't be treated the way they are and that the relationship isn't a good one. But the trade-off of feeling intense emotions outweighs that little nagging voice.

In the story above, I mentioned that our friend didn't get the feedback from those around her who had concerns about her relationship. But guess what? She had those very same concerns. The early relationship was exciting and she was caught up in the romance of it all (which is really easy to do). But as time went by she saw things that concerned her. Instead of calling him out and addressing them with her boyfriend, she was swept along by emotion.

So they got engaged, and then she was occupied with all the planning that comes along with preparing for a wedding. It was a rush to be planning for such a special day. During that time she continued to have mild concerns but took that as a normal, cold-feet feeling.

On her wedding day the feelings flooded in and she knew that she shouldn't go through with the marriage. But she did anyhow. She ignored that little voice even though it spoke louder and louder, and she went through with a marriage that ended very badly just a short time later.

From time to time in a developing relationship, you have to rise above the excitement and emotion of it all and ask yourself some difficult questions. And you have a responsibility to listen to that still small voice and be honest about your thoughts and doubts.

Simply put, you have to pay attention to the red flags. It can be easy to blow them off because you are in love and feel strongly about that person. But you have to be able to step back and engage your brain. He doesn't want kids and you do—it may seem like an issue that you can work out later, but maybe it's not and it will become a real pitfall in your relationship. You want to live near family but she wants to move far away—maybe you can figure it out later, but later is going to sneak up on you sooner than you think and this issue might throw you into a relational tailspin.

I can't say this strongly enough: a red flag is a red flag! Engage your brain, be honest with yourself and with those who love you, and make your decisions based on something other than your emotions and attraction. If you don't, you are going to pay for it. There's no other way around it.

THE NEXT STEP

What's the point of all this work? Well, many people get caught up in serious relationships with people they really don't know all that well. They end up engaged and married only to find out important stuff that they should have learned sooner. The hope is that this book helped you get to know your significant other, to get comfortable with asking and answering questions, and to create an appropriate level of disclosure at every step of the way. All of this will lead to greater relational health, and if things do move forward, you'll at least know who you're involved with and what comes with it.

Keep in mind that you haven't asked these questions for the purpose of finding fault—although you definitely will. No one is perfect and no one can meet every expectation (not even you). The point is to know someone, faults and all, and to be able to objectively weigh whether those faults are so great as to scare you off. Certainly good relationships occur between two people who are less than perfect.

If your significant other wasn't willing to enter into this process of discovery—if he or she gave you shallow or lame answers to your questions or was closed off, secretive, or overly sensitive—ask yourself why someone who supposedly cares for you would act this way. A person who does not want to be known is a person who may cause you heartbreak down the line.

Enjoy and continue this process of discovery, both about yourself and the person you care about. Doing so makes for a rewarding experience and a lasting, solid, and informed relationship.

REFLECTION QUESTIONS

1. What important things have you observed about your significant other? How did you make these observations?

2. Which trusted friends or family members could you solicit feedback from about this significant relationship? (If you say *no one*, that's a red flag.)

3. Have you ever taken the time to get away, to be quiet and still, and to really reflect on this important relationship? If so, what did you hear and how do you plan to act on it? If not, would you consider doing so? (If you say *no*, that's a red flag.)

4. What is one thing you have learned about yourself as a result of being in this relationship?

Want more?

Even when you communicate successfully, marriage can still take you by surprise. *Happily Ever After* will help you establish realistic expectations and goals for marriage through stimulating questions, journal pages, and honest personal stories.